Dr. Thomas Mathews
(1944 - 2005)

(i)

Vision, Mission And A Movement

ISBN 81-8284-013-9

(Portions of this book in their original form previously published under the title 'He Saw a Man Named Mathews'.)

Scripture quotations, unless otherwise noted, are from the New American Standard Version of the Bible.

Published by Native Missionary Movement
821 Vinecrest Lane, Richardson, TX 75080

In India:
Native Missionary Movement
Church Road, Sanjay Park
Udaipur, Rajasthan 313 004
Email: contact@nmmindia.org

Printed at Cross & Crown Offset Press, Udaipur, (Raj.) INDIA

Vision,

Mission

And

A Movement

The story of Thomas Mathews and
the Native Missionary Movement of India

Roger Simmons

Dedication

I am the one in the village.
I am the one who is poor.
I am the one who is needy.
Who will appear at my door?

Who will provide me a morsel?
Give me a drink from a well?
Clothes for my tired, naked body?
Words that will save me from hell?

This book is dedicated to the millions in India who are waiting
in darkness to hear the name, Yishu (Jesus).

Contents

Acknowledgements
Preface
Introduction

Part One: A Man, A Vision, A Mission

One	: The Birth of a Missionary	1
Two	: Childhood Years	5
Three	: Years of Discontent	9
Four	: A New Direction	17
Five	: To the North	21
Six	: Land of Destiny	25
Seven	: Summer HeatWinter Chills	31
Eight	: Cries of Faith	37
Nine	: Mary and Marriage	45
Ten	: Northward Together	53
Eleven:	: In Perils of the Gentiles	63

Part Two: A Movement

Twelve	: The Beginnings of a Movement	69
Thirteen	: Kingdom Women	75
Fourteen	: Manohar Bhawan	79
Fifteen	: Filadelfia Bible College	85
Sixteen	: Highways and Byways	97
Seventeen	: Labor On: A Time of Growth	103
Eighteen	: Spend and Be Spent: A Time of Grief	117

Part Three: Native Missionary Movement Today

Nineteen	: India Today	125
Twenty	: NMM: Love in Action	131

Part Four: The Challenge Ahead

Twenty-one	: Suffering Saints	155
Twenty-two	: Danger Ahead	165
Twenty-three	: A Call to Compassion	177
Twenty-four	: Epilogue	191
Twenty-five	: A Call to Commitment	195

Acknowledgements

The Spirit of Christ combined the efforts of many different people to bring this volume to fruition.

- ❏ Jon Thollander wrote the original work titled, "He Saw a Man Named Mathews" based on interviews with the late Rev. Thomas Mathews.

- ❏ Roger Simmons rewrote that text and added material that was not covered in the original work. His wife, Linda, provided invaluable service in typing and proofreading.

- ❏ Christy Osborne, James and Mary Pearce, Jessica Simmons, and Joy and Grace Punnoose graciously reviewed the manuscript and gave valuable input.

- ❏ Countless numbers strengthened the project through prayer. A sincere "Thank you" is extended to them for their devotion to the Lord and His people.

- ❏ Finally, thank you to all the believers who are a part of the Native Missionary Movement team. This is your story.

Preface

This is a story about the love of God for His people in North India. It is the story of a man, the late Thomas Mathews. It is the story of his vision and the mission on which that vision led him.

This is the story of a movement the Native Missionary Movement of India. This part of the story is still being played out, for the vision of Thomas Mathews has unfolded into a dynamic undertaking that has spawned more than a thousand missionaries who have the same vision; and it continues today.

This is the story of North India and its people at once a land of enchantment, and a land of darkness. It is a story of the Great Light that has dawned for hundreds of thousands who live in that land.

This is a story about North America and its people, for they play a pivotal role in its last chapters. Prepare to be challenged, not only by the lives of the indigenous Indians, but also by the call of God to your own heart and vision as well.

Introduction

Kerala. That name doesn't mean much to most people in the Western Hemisphere. It's a state in southern India, a little smaller in size than the combined area of Vermont and New Hampshire. Located on the western tip of the Indian peninsula, the waves of the Arabian Sea wash upon its beautiful beaches. Full of rivers and lakes, rainforests and lush green rice fields, it is known today for its rubber plantations and coconut palm groves.

But Kerala (say CARE uh luh) is also known by those Indians who name the Name of Jesus as the heartland of Christianity in India. For it was to the people of Kerala 2,000 years ago that the apostle Thomas shared the glorious news of the One whom he no longer doubted. And it was from its people 2,000 years later that God would send the son of a poor, believing factory worker to bring the same message to thousands upon thousands of lost souls in northern India.

Church historians believe that after Pentecost, Thomas reached the shores of Kerala via the Arabian Sea. Through his ministry a large number of high-caste Hindus in southern India embraced Christianity before he was martyred in 52 A.D. Eventually, a thriving Christian community took root.

It was in this southern state of Kerala that the story of the Native Missionary Movement of India began.

PART ONE:

A MAN,
A VISION,
A MISSION

Chapter One

The Birth of a Missionary

In the last years of British rule in India, M. Chacko and his wife, Rachel, moved from their native city, Mundiapally, to the small town of Punalur in Kerala to start a pioneer Gospel work. Living only by faith, they rented a small, simple house with mud walls and a roof thatched with coconut palm leaves. They decided on this budding industrial town because a new paper mill was being built there, and many people from all over the region were moving in. At the time, the Chackos were the only Gospel workers in Punalur.

Often, Pastor Chacko and Rachel went without food for many days. With no one to help them and no support or assistance coming from outside, they lived in hardship day after day. But they trusted in the Lord for their daily needs, and resolutely went about their ministry.

Early each morning, the couple set off to share the love of Christ and pray for the sick. One morning, after walking several miles, Chacko and Rachel came to the house of a man named Mathai. Now Mathai's ancestors were very traditional orthodox Christians. Mathai and his family had recently moved to Punalur to work in the paper mill. His twenty-four-year-old son, Thomas, worked there as well to help support the family. But on this day

Thomas lay inside the house, dying of typhoid fever—a fatal illness for many at that time. He had already been bedridden for over two weeks.

Upon learning of Thomas' condition, Pastor Chacko asked Mathai if he could talk to him. He walked to the bedside where Thomas lay, half-delirious with fever, pain, and weakness. In gentle tones he told him of the saving love and the healing power of Christ. Thomas opened his eyes a bit, looked up feebly from his bed, and murmured, "If the Lord will heal me from this sickness, all my life I will live for Him."

The pastor laid his hands on the sick young man struggling between life and death, and he prayed for him, rebuking the sickness. Then he and his wife left.

But something wonderful took place in Mathai's home. As soon as the pastor left the house, the fever left Thomas and he was able to sit up. In a while he got out of bed and ate some food.

The next morning the pastor came back to see how he was doing. As he approached the door, Thomas ran out to him and exclaimed, "I want to come to your prayer meeting!" Chacko was surprised and overjoyed that God had healed this young man, and he was blessed that Thomas showed an interest in the God who healed him.

Soon Thomas went back to his job in the paper mill, and in time God completely restored his health. Chacko returned several times to Mathai's home and prayed with the family. In time the whole family believed in Jesus as their Savior, and they became the first fruits in the ministry of Pastor Chacko and his wife.

Even while they were struggling, the Chackos kept on gladly serving their Lord, and He rewarded their faith as He had promised: *"Let us not lose heart in doing good, for in due time we will reap, if we do not grow weary"* (Galatians 6:9). Little did they know how far those first fruits they reaped would spread.

At the same time, there lived in Kerala a man named N.V. Varghese. He, too, had heard about the Lord Jesus Christ, and he accepted Him as his personal Savior. His wife and their seven children also became believers, soon after. But when his friends and relatives heard about what Varghese had done, they began to ostracize him. Before long they demanded that he and his family leave their village. So this humble family left their relatives, their friends—everything that had been a part of their lives. After traveling many weary miles on bullock carts loaded with their meager possessions, they came to a farming town located near Punalur. They were poor, but hard working and faithful to the Lord, and they were excited about their new location and their new salvation.

They decided to settle there, and right away Varghese began going from house to house, praying for sick people and witnessing for the Lord. He had a great deal of compassion for the suffering and the sick, especially those with smallpox, for in those days there was a terrible smallpox epidemic. No one else dared to go near those afflicted with this dread disease to nurse them back to health, for fear of catching it themselves.

The Lord had an additional reason for leading the Vargheses to Punalur. The Vargheses had a daughter named Mariamma, who loved the Lord. In time, a marriage was proposed between Mariamma and Mathai's son, Thomas—the same young man who was healed in body and saved in spirit through the prayer of Pastor Chacko.

Now in India, it is the custom for a family member or a religious leader to arrange a marriage. After a few weeks the proposal was settled, the marriage date fixed, and Thomas and Mariamma were soon married.

Three happy years went by, but no children had yet come to Thomas and Mariamma, even though they had been praying and crying before God for a little one. However, they never lost hope, believing that the God of hope could perform a miracle in their family and give them a child. Frequent meetings and prayers were held in their house for them.

One day the Mathews' invited a prophetess named Annamma to come and pray for them. As they prayed, the Holy Spirit gave a prophecy to Annamma for the childless couple. She spoke in the Holy Spirit: "God is going to give you a son, like He gave Isaac to Abraham and Sarah. You must bring him up for *His* ministry. He will provide for all his needs, and He will be his inheritance."

"If God will give us a son, we will dedicate him for God's ministry," was the young couple's heartfelt response.

God moved quickly, and within a year the Lord fulfilled His promise. A son, Thomas, was born to them on February 9, 1944. The parents were so overjoyed that they called the child "Joy" in their home. After two months Pastor Chacko dedicated the child in a Sunday service. Thomas and Mariamma were grateful to God—and they were determined to fulfill their promise to Him.

Chapter Two

Childhood Years

Young Thomas was brought up in a God-fearing home. His parents were very active in the church, and they greatly respected God's servants. Whenever his father met any traveling preacher on the road, he would bring him home, feed him, and give him lodging for a day or two.

During his school years Thomas proved to be a very capable, hard-working student. He had accepted Christ as his Savior early on, and he was, at first, a very pious boy. Until the eighth grade he studied in a Catholic school, but it had only a bit of true Christian influence. He excelled in his Sunday school class, and he had a good, general knowledge of the Bible; but eventually he lost interest in going to church.

Several years after Pastor Chacko left Punalur, another pastor, V. T. Koshy, came to town. Koshy was very good at working with young people, and every summer he would conduct a daily youth Bible study. Thomas' parents often asked him to attend, but he never wanted to go. However, this pastor understood the situation and was very tactful.

Koshy had been given a brand new green Raleigh bicycle made in England to use in his ministry. One day he came to the

Mathews' home to talk with Joy. As they visited, he said, "If you come to the Bible study, I will let you ride my bicycle for awhile after class each day."

Now Thomas—or "Mathews" as his friends called him[1]— was fascinated with bicycles, like most thirteen year-old boys. So he went, but only to ride that bike. He studied the Bible three hours every morning; then when everyone else had gone home, Mathews got the key to the bike, and he would pedal it all over town the whole afternoon.

A year or two later, Mathews learned about a summer Bible memory contest. As an extra incentive, the pastor offered a Malayalam[2] Bible to anyone who could recite one thousand Bible verses from memory. The cost of a Bible was four rupees (about ten cents), a large sum to a boy.

Winning the contest and the Bible represented quite a challenge, but Mathews had a good memory, and he liked challenges. He studied long, and soon he memorized about 1,500 verses, 1,000 of which he could recite by heart with confidence.

On the day of the contest, thirty-five nervous young people stood in a line. Each one would recite a verse; then they would go to the second round, and everyone would attempt another verse, and so on. Contestants who made a mistake or who could not think of a verse to say had to drop out of the competition. The contest began, and after four hours, all were eliminated but two— Mathews and his good friend, Johny.

Two hours later Mathews and Johny came to the 999th verse. They had been at it for six hours. Johny had to go first. Five minutes were given to say the verse, but as the final seconds ticked away, he remained silent: he had no verses left.

Finally he murmured, "I surrender."

Mathews then correctly recited another verse, and since he wanted the Bible, he recited one more—number *one thousand*.

Both first place in the competition and the beautiful Malayalam Bible were his.

Although Mathews excelled at studying and memorizing the Bible, deep in his heart he had neither a fear of God nor any real commitment to the Lord. His grandfather was an evangelist, and he often told Mathews that doing God's work was the best thing any man could do. Mathews' earliest memory of the Scriptures came from him. When he was younger he had thought, "What a great thing it would be to work with my own hands and never depend on anybody and serve the Lord and the people, like my grandfather."

But now he had no desire to be a minister. He was a brilliant student and was looking ahead to an academic degree and a good-paying job.

Chapter Three

Years of Discontent

$\mathcal{M}$athews progressed through high school, but his Christian testimony regressed. He had managed to keep most of his feelings inside, but inevitably his rebellion surfaced; and this change did not go unnoticed by his parents. They soon realized that he was going to church only to please them.

His mother warned him, "You need to serve the Lord. We dedicated you to His ministry."

I can serve God with my money, he thought, thinking ahead to a successful career after college. But in his heart he carried another reason for ignoring his mother's advice: simply put, he hated preachers. From his point of view there were very few sincere preachers like his grandfather, and he felt that many preachers preached only for money. In addition, he saw pastors, and other Christians as well, who had little or no positive influence on others.

The Communist government came to power in Kerala in 1957, when Mathews was in the seventh grade, and he then began to develop a secret attraction to communistic ideals—an attraction that his parents were not aware of. Punalur had become a breeding ground of communist activity because of the big paper mill and the thousands of naïve laborers in its trade union. Communist speakers often came and gave fiery speeches. Although many well-known Christian speakers also came to town, Mathews went to hear the Communist speakers instead. He found in them a fire, a commitment, and a passion for their ideology that was missing in the lives of most Christians.

Mathews' mother grew fearful of the change she saw developing in him, and again she tearfully reminded him, "Son, before you were born we dedicated you to God's glorious ministry. Don't rebel against God. God will get you! God will catch you!"

But the advice and prayers of his dear mother did not have any effect on this growing young man. Over time he developed friendships with people who led him astray from his spiritual moorings.

Mathews graduated from high school with very high honors, and his father wanted to send him to the best college in Kerala. The only university in the state was in the capital city, Trivandrum, and it was very difficult to gain admission. But even though there was a college in his hometown of Punalur, his father borrowed enough money for Mathews to pursue his studies in physics at the big university.

For two years he studied at Trivandrum, and he was very successful—first in his class. But still he had no faith in the Lord. His mother wrote letters every week. She told him that he did not fear God, that his heart wasn't right with Him, and that he was only bluffing his parents. But she also reaffirmed her commitment to him: "I will not give up on you! I will cry to the Lord and fast and pray until God gets you, until God catches you."

However, Mathews wrote back to her, "Mother, don't waste your time fasting. Eat well and then pray."

She had become very thin because of her fasting, and this made Mathews even more rebellious. He thought, *What is this? My mother should eat well. And what is there to 'catch me' about? I have never cheated anyone; I have never committed any immoral act.*

Now that he was attending the university in Trivandrum, he still liked the Communist people and read all the Communist literature—and he saw nothing wrong with it. When a well-known preacher would come to town, Mathews would go to hear him preach, but he wouldn't commit himself to Christ. He was not anti-Christian, but he wanted something real to live for.

Into the Deep

After his sophomore year at the university, Mathews and a group of his friends decided to go to a summer vacation youth camp in the beautiful mountains of Kerala, which were full of rivers and picnic spots. Even though it was a Christian youth camp, Mathews and his friends set off; not for spiritual fellowship, but simply to have some fun, meet new people, and see new places.

Nearly five hundred excited young people gathered together for the opening meeting. The Holy Spirit touched many of them as they sang songs of praise and listened intently to the powerful preaching. Mathews and his friends were also present.

At the end of that first meeting, the camp leader made a special announcement: "Young friends, those of you who have come from far away places; I want to give you a warning. There is a big river below the camp called the Pampa, and some of you may want to go there to swim. A big rock rises out of the water just off an old church. Let that rock serve as a warning sign. There is a powerful whirlpool at that spot, and you will be caught in it if you go near, and you will never return. I warn you again: Don't swim near that rock!"

Now Mathews, who liked challenges, had the attitude that if anyone told him to do something, then he didn't want to do it; and if anyone told him *not* to do something, then that was what he wanted to do. So when this proud young rebel heard the warning, he instantly determined to swim in that spot. He thought, *Who is this man, telling us not to go to a certain spot on the river? He didn't purchase the whole river! We are campers, we are free, and we can swim anywhere. Who can stop us?*

After the meeting he boasted to his friends: "Tomorrow morning we will go there and take a swim, and we'll show everyone that we can do it!"

Early the next morning Mathews and his friends made their way down to the river, while the other campers were assembling for the morning meeting. Mathews led as usual, but the others followed uncertainly behind. He marched along the Pampa, straight to the old church and the rock that the campers had been warned about. Now as this river came down from the mountains, it took a 90-degree turn at that spot, which created a powerful whirlpool.

He jumped in and waded out confidently a few feet; but suddenly he disappeared, right at the spot where a steep drop-off fell into the swirling water. Mathews was caught in the current, and he could not touch the bottom with his feet. Spinning around, he fought against the undercurrents, and as he did he could tell that he was being sucked underneath the rocks. He valiantly struggled to the surface and cried out to his friends standing close by on the bank, "I'm dying!...I'm drowning!...This is real!...Come on guys, save me! Come!...Come!"

But his terrified friends, seeing the fear of impending death on the face of the sinking young man, did not dare to jump into the water. They were yelling and crying as he went down again. Only bubbles of water were visible above, but Mathews was fighting against death below.

Meanwhile the rest of the campers had all gathered back at the campground, and the first session was just beginning. As they were singing, suddenly someone dashed to the stage and cried, "A young man is drowning in the river!" The sound of singing quickly faded, and many of the young people rushed out of the meeting and down the hill to the riverbank to see what was happening.

When they came to the dreaded rock, a crowd of villagers who lived nearby had already gathered. One of them shouted to the campers, "One boy is gone—let *him* go! Don't try to save him. If anybody else falls into this spot, he will die as well. No one who has fallen in here has ever come back alive!"

Another cried out, "There is a curse on this place. Every year someone drowns here, and already this year another boy has drowned. Let him go. It was his turn. Nobody else should try to save him, or two will die instead of one!"

As the horror-stricken crowd watched, Mathews fought his way to the surface one more time, gasping for air. But by now he was almost unconscious, and all hope of survival seemed gone. As he slowly spiraled toward the bottom of the river for the last time, the words his mother had written to him flashed through his mind: *Son, I am fasting and praying for you so that God may catch you.*

Semi-conscious and close to death, he cried out in his spirit, *Oh God of my mother, I know You are alive and You answer prayers. I rebelled against You; I never lived for You. But if You will save me from this death, the rest of my days I will live for You with all of my strength. I will work for You, Lord. Save my life from death. Give me life to serve You.* And as he prayed, Mathews sank to the bottom.

But just as Jesus heard Peter's cry on the angry sea, the Lord heard Mathews' prayer uttered from the depths of that river. Up at the camp, a young man named George Mathew (no relation) had also heard the cries and yelling coming from the river. He, too, ran down the hill, and as he neared the bank he knew instinctively that someone was drowning because of the shrieking and crying of the onlookers. George, an excellent swimmer, had never even seen the drowning boy, much less met him; but he plunged into the swirling current anyway, heedless of the shouts and cries of warning.

Wasting no time, George forced his way downward, groping about blindly in the darkness of the turbulent waters. As he neared the bottom, his hands found Mathews, and he grabbed onto him tightly—like an umbilical cord between life and death. With all his strength he pulled him up to the surface and dragged him out onto the riverbank. Yes, Jesus heard Mathews' cry, and He reached out and saved him just in time!

Someone in the crowd turned him upside down to clear the water from his lungs. He was then carried up to the camp and laid in a room to recover, so exhausted that he couldn't talk or even open his eyes.

Mathews rested for several hours. When he had recovered sufficiently to come to the auditorium, the meeting resumed. The speaker that day was a preacher from Kerala, Pastor P. M. Philip; and Mathews, in spite of his harrowing experience, listened intently to the message.

Just as the preacher was concluding, Mathews quietly asked if he could give his testimony. Everyone was eager to hear him, so he stood up and walked slowly and unsteadily to the stage. Before all the people he spoke quietly: "I came here for fun and to enjoy time with my friends. I didn't want anything to do with spiritual things. Then I met death face to face—and God met me. And now my mother's prayers are answered. I am going home to tell my parents what happened; then, I will go to North India. Now I have only one ambition—to take the name of Jesus to North India: to go there, to live there, and to die there. I have left all other ambitions behind. I have forsaken all my dreams to become great in the world."

As he spoke, there was a breathless silence in the room. Many of the campers had tears in their eyes. When he finished, several shouted "Hallelujah!"

At the end of the meeting Mathews left his friends, and he left his old way of life. He packed his belongings, got on a bus, and returned home. When he met his parents, he related to them all that had happened. They could see in his face that a change had come into his heart; and when he finished the story, they both hugged him, with tears of joy and thankfulness to God streaming down their cheeks.

He explained that he had been called to go to Rajasthan in northern India, leaving everything, including his studies, behind. After he shared this vision with his parents, they encouraged him saying, "Since God has called you to go there, don't worry about what people say. Obey the voice of God and He will take care of you. We have no greater joy than to see you go as a missionary to the North."

The South and the North

It needs to be understood at this point that, to the people of India, the dividing line between northern and southern India is somewhat geographic. The four southern states—Kerala, Tamil Nadu, Karnataka, and Andhra Pradesh—are clustered together at the bottom of the country, while the greater land area and number of states lies to the north and northeast.

But the overriding distinction between the two regions centers on cultural and social issues. The South has always had more educational opportunities, prosperity, employment, and cleanliness than the more heavily populated North. In addition, the South has always had a Christian presence.

Therefore, for Mathews to have received his parents' blessing to go to the North was remarkable, due to the fact that most Christians in the South did not consider northern India a desirable place to do mission work. In many respects it was the same as going to a foreign country. The climate, the religion, the dress, the food, and the language—all were different. Few southerners went to the North as missionaries and stayed, and only a few of those had even a little success from their efforts.

Mathews had been totally transformed. All that he had learned in the past from his parents and his church now became intensely real to him. From that time on he was always ready to testify to the saving power of prayer.

During his high school years Mathews had read *Through Gates of Splendor*, by Elizabeth Elliot. Its pages recount the deeply touching story of Jim Elliot, the author's husband, and his four fellow missionaries, who all sacrificed their lives to win the Auca tribe in Ecuador to Christ. Earlier Jim had written these words in his journal: "He is no fool who gives what he cannot keep to gain that which he cannot lose."

Now, after his near-tragic drowning experience, Mathews clearly understood the meaning of what Jim Elliot had written: In order to gain souls for eternity, a man must first give up his *own* life, which he cannot keep for himself forever anyway. In the words of Jesus, "He who loves his life will lose it, and he who hates his life in this world [for the sake of Jesus and His Gospel] will keep it for eternal life" (John 12:25).

Chapter Four

A New Direction

*M*athews knew that his entire family endured hard times in order for him to go to college. There was very little income, and his father had borrowed money from his friends to pay for Mathews' education. In the Indian culture it is expected that the oldest son will contribute to the family's welfare, if that becomes necessary. So it would have been reasonable for his parents to expect that he would follow suit.

But his parents told him that, even though in the past they had dreamed he would complete college, get a job, and help his father get out of debt, they were certain that God had called him to go to the North. "We are praying for you," they told him. "Don't worry, God will take care of us. He has called you for His glorious ministry; so don't look back. Take the Word of God and go wherever the Lord sends you. We will work hard and try to help you as much as we can. For the rest of your needs, look to God. He is faithful. The God of Elijah will feed you, too."

In the following days and weeks, God tested Mathews on worrying about "what people say," as his parents had warned. It was a hard time for him, because his friends and his teachers persisted in trying to convince him to continue his studies. Even some pastors who came and prayed for him said, "Why don't

you complete your degree? Then you can serve the Lord better."
But he answered that he had made a commitment to the Lord,
and that he could not break his word to Him.

Now South India had many churches and preachers, because
of the early Christian influence. But North India was an open
mission field. Very few preachers and missionaries went to the
North, and among the hundreds of millions of people there,
only a handful had been won for Christ. More than 85 percent
were Hindus; the rest were either followers of Islam or some
other religion.

Mathews had learned in earlier years from pastors and
visiting preachers that Rajasthan, a desert state on the border of
Pakistan in northwest India, was the most difficult area of all to
reach. He now had a compelling burden from God in his heart to
go to the most difficult place in North India and spend every day
working for the Lord. He thought, *God saved me from death,
and I will live all my life for Him. I will serve Jesus, the One who
saved my life, in the hardest place.* Rajasthan was that "hardest
place."

After the camp experience he began to read his Bible as if
he had never read it before, even though he knew more than a
thousand verses by heart. The Bible became so real and so sweet
to him that he never wanted to put it down. On one occasion,
going without food, he spent three days doing nothing but
praying and reading his Bible (the same Malayalam Bible that he
had won several years earlier).

One day he received a telegram from P.M. Philip, the speaker
at the summer youth camp, asking him to come to a four-month
Bible study program at the Shalom Bible School in Kottayam,
Kerala. Mathews gladly accepted the invitation and enrolled in
the school. During the term, an evangelist from Rajasthan named
K. V. Philip came as a guest speaker. He shared with the students
about his sufferings in Rajasthan—the same place where
Mathews was determined to serve the Lord.

That afternoon, as K.V. was leaving to travel back to his home, Mathews ran after him. When he caught up with him, Mathews breathlessly pledged, "I will come to Rajasthan. I've been praying to God, and now I know where I am going."

But Philip surprised him when he stated, "You will not come. Nobody goes there."

Mathews quickly returned: "Yes I will. You'll see!" Then Philip left.

Mathews soon completed the Bible course, and Pastor P.M. Philip prayed for him and blessed him in his life's mission. Then he returned to Punalur to bid farewell to his parents and prepare to leave.

When the awaited day arrived, believers from the Punalur church were gathered in his home to bid him goodbye, filled with different emotions. Some were wondering why this young man would abruptly leave his studies. Others were excited that someone from their own church would be willing to go as the first missionary from their part of Kerala to North India.

The believers prayed for him, and several people gave him small gifts. An old, godly mother in the church gave him a used, metal suitcase to carry his things, which were few in number: one extra set of clothes, his Bible, and a few other small items. His grandfather prayed for him and blessed him.

Before Mathews left, his mother said to him, "You know we have always welcomed God's servants from any Christian denomination into our home, and anyone who passed our way carrying a Bible was always invited in. Our God will be faithful to you, too. He will provide you with food when you are hungry and a place to sleep when you are tired. We have committed you to the Lord's Hand, and according to His promise, He will take care of you."

With all these blessings, gifts, and prayers, on April 5, 1963, at nineteen years of age, Thomas Mathews left the place where he grew up.

Chapter Five

To The North

$\mathcal{T}$he day Mathews departed, he traveled only fifty miles north to Kottayam, the site of the Bible school he attended. Kottayam was also the home of his mentor and teacher, Pastor Philip, and Mathews wanted to bid him farewell.

He arrived at the pastor's house, and they visited for a while. After praying for him, the pastor placed one hundred rupees[3] in his hand and said, "This is for you. God will provide the rest." Then he said goodbye.

Mathews' initial destination in northern India was the capital city, Delhi. Many years before, a missionary from Kerala, M.K. Chacko,[4] had gone to serve the Lord in Delhi. He had visited Mathews' church in Punalur several times when Mathews was a boy, and he would narrate his stories of faith—how God fed him and his family and protected them. Mathews wanted to visit Pastor Chacko and learn all he could from this man's years of experience before he went to Rajasthan.

So he purchased a train ticket to Delhi for his first journey away from Kerala. With tears in his eyes, a vision for North India in his heart, and a firm conviction that the Lord had called him to be an evangelist and missionary to the North Indian people, he stepped onto the train to follow his Master's calling into an unknown future. The cocky, boastful college boy was left behind in the past. The fledgling evangelist and missionary to the lost people of northern India set his face to the unknown.

The train pulled out of the station and unhurriedly made its way northward. On the fourth day out, after nearly 1,500 miles, it finally drew into the sprawling city of Delhi.[5] Traffic-clogged streets lined with bazaars gave way to a skyline dominated by the domes and minarets of the Great Mosque. Not far away stood the imposing Red Fort, the palace of India's bygone Mughal emperors.

As he stepped off the train, Mathews was immediately made aware of the cultural differences between his home and this land so far away. He felt rather conspicuous, wearing his native *dhoti* (a cotton wrap-around) and a shirt; for all the other men and boys around him wore pants!

Pastor Chacko met him at the station, and the two of them wound their way through the maze of street vendors and shoppers to Chacko's home. His two-week stay with the missionary gave Mathews his first lessons in living by simple trust in the Lord, for this pioneer to the Hindi-speaking people was a great man of faith.

Chacko only spoke Hindi, the language of the North—not the Malayalam of his native Kerala. Mathews began learning Hindi from the pastor, and he also learned to eat chapati, a flatbread made of wheat, similar to a tortilla. Chapatis are to the northerners what rice is to those in the South—the staple food of their diet. Pastor Chacko was convinced that it was essential to identify with the indigenous people in every way possible, if working for Christ was to have any success.

One day Chacko told Mathews something very sobering: "Many young people have come to stay with me from Kerala saying that they want to work for the Lord in North India. But in time, when they find that they cannot get the food of Kerala here, many of them leave. Are you also like that?"

Mathews didn't hesitate. He said, "No."

Then Mathews narrated the details of his near-drowning experience and said, "The Lord snatched me from death, and I am ready to accept any kind of life. I have no choice. I must be like the North Indians. I will eat what the North Indians eat, and I will speak what the North Indians speak. I won't go back. I cannot."

Pastor Chacko replied, "Here is a test. If you can leave your rice-eating habit and your Malayalam tongue, and if, instead, you can eat chapati and speak Hindi while you are with me these few days, then I will be able to tell whether you will stay in the North or not."

Mathews was determined. From that moment on he began to adopt the North Indian food and the Hindi language as his own.

For fifteen days Mathews stayed there. These were very precious days for two reasons: first, because Chacko's testimony and prayer life challenged him; and second, because he witnessed faith in action, seeing how to trust in God for everything.

On the day he left, Pastor Chacko prayed for him and sent him on his way. Mathews had passed the test.

Chapter Six

Land of Destiny

The train crept through the countryside of Rajasthan, and on both sides of the track Mathews observed with keen interest the Rajasthani people working on their farms. Tall men with red or orange turbans to protect themselves from the heat, and women clad in colorful skirts and blouses, their heads and faces covered with transparent veils, labored in the fields or fed cattle, camels, and sheep.

As the miles rolled along, Mathews fell in love with these people. He knew that they were the reason why God had saved him from death, and that God sent him to them. These people were now his people, and Rajasthan was his promised land. This was the land of his destiny.

He thought, *These are the people I will live with all my life. These are the people God wants me to serve. I will live for them, work for them, and teach them. I am for them.*

The history of Rajasthan thrilled Mathews, especially the history of Udaipur and the Rajputs. The Rajputs had fought against the Mughals, the conquerors, centuries before, and were renowned for their bravery. Into this land of the brave the Lord had sent him, and he, too, purposed in his heart to be brave for the Lord.

Mathews arrived in Udaipur in April of 1963. Udaipur, "city of sunrise", was then a small town of 60,000 people—small on India's scale, that is. There were bigger cities in Rajasthan without any evangelists, but he felt that God had sent him to this particular place.

K.V. Philip, the speaker at the Bible school who tried to discourage Mathews, greeted him as he stepped down from the train. There were no auto rickshaws or taxis at the time, so they carried his few belongings and walked on and on until they reached K.V.'s room.

Philip explained that he had been in Udaipur for two years, but with hardly any success. Only South Indians who lived in the area attended his small church; there were no native Rajasthanis. Weary from his apparently fruitless labor, he wanted to go to Jodhpur, a much larger city also in Rajasthan, and begin a work there.

Mathews started working alongside Philip, with the aid of some of the other southerners. One of his first tasks was learning the Hindi language. It came rapidly to him in a short time, and he almost left Malayalam behind. He concentrated on the task of winning the North for Christ so well that he never looked back to the past. Worries about his parents or his studies were left behind as well, knowing that God would take care of those matters.

Bicycles were the essential mode of transportation in the region. However, Mathews did not have one of his own when he arrived, so at first he sat on the back of K.V.'s bicycle as they made their rounds. But before long, his spiritual mentor from the South, P.M. Philip, sent Mathews two hundred rupees, with which he purchased his own bike.

On most days Mathews and K.V. packed up big bundles of Hindi tracts and Gospels, together with some chapatis and pickles, and peddled off to the villages in the early mornings.

Sometimes they traveled as far as thirty miles in a day, stopping only to rest and eat their small lunch under a tree that grew near some water. When they came to a village, they shared the Gospel from house to house, covering as many as three or four villages in a day. Then they returned home late at night.

When they entered the villages, they didn't say to the people, "Here's a Bible for you," or "Come and hear the message of Christ." The villagers didn't know what a Bible was or anything about Jesus. So they did what the village postman did. Reaching a village, they cried out, "You have a letter! Come. Come. Here is your letter." This is what the postman would shout from his bicycle when he came with mail, and the people would crowd around him.

When they saw the evangelists with their big bundles, the villagers came over to them. Then Mathews and Philip handed them tracts and Gospels, saying, "This is not a letter from any man; this is a letter from God."

The villagers took them gladly. Children rushed back to their homes shouting, "God's letter from heaven is here!" However a few clever fellows, after skimming through a Gospel, called out, "What is this? You are cheating and bluffing us!"

The missionaries told them that it was a good, spiritual book. "This book is full of wisdom and good advice. If you read this and follow its teachings, you will have peace in your mind, and blessing and prosperity will come to your family." After hearing this, the villagers received the Gospels and tracts with respect and went back to their homes.

Ninety-five percent of villagers in Rajasthan were illiterate, so they couldn't benefit directly from either the Gospels or the tracts Mathews and Philip brought. Even today, many still cannot read or write. However, these people didn't throw any of the printed material away. Instead, they tucked it into the tiles of their roofs, hoping that someday, someone would come to them who could read. If that happened they would give the Bible or the tract to him and beg, "Please read this letter for us. Someone came here and gave us this letter from God. What does it say?" Then that person would read it for them. Later, most of them would ask that person to write to the contact address for more information.

Mathews and Philip pedaled one day to a village school and asked the headmaster if they could share something about peace with the children and read Bible stories to them. The headmaster said, "Okay, come and tell us what Christmas is." Then all of the students gathered together in an open area and sat on the ground. Mathews and Philip tenderly shared the eternal story of God's love: how Jesus was born, how He lived, how He died, and how He rose again. Then the two evangelists passed out free Gospels to all the students and the teacher as well.

However, this same tactic was not always met with such an open response. Once in a while a headmaster hostile toward anything other than his own religion would shout at the two, "Why don't you preach from our scriptures? We have our holy books. We have our gods and goddesses. Why don't you preach about them?"

On such occasions Mathews lacked anything to say in response. God was testing him and showing him that he still had much to learn about sharing the Gospel to people living in this stronghold of Hinduism.

Still disappointed because he could not break through to the local people, K.V. Philip left Udaipur for the city of Jodhpur a few months after Mathews arrived. But he was a very sincere, zealous young evangelist, and Mathews appreciated their experiences while together.[6]

Now that Mathews was all alone in Udaipur, he knew that he faced the same predicament that had driven Philip away. Before Philip left, he had encouraged the newcomer to go to Jaipur, the capital city of Rajasthan, with a population of over one million. Jaipur, 250 miles to the northeast, was without any evangelists. He told Mathews, "I worked very hard here for more than two years, but nobody listens. It is better for you to go to a bigger city because you are an educated man, and they would appreciate you. You could plant a big church there. Don't waste your life in this small town."

"No," Mathews stated, "Whatever happens, I will stay here in Udaipur. I will spend my life here." Challenges didn't deter him; he was where God wanted him to be.

When Philip left he gave Mathews his old room. The rent was only fifteen rupees a month, but for the first three months Mathews couldn't pay even that small amount. He collected a few rupees here and there selling Gospel literature. But when he visited homes to share the Gospel, they wouldn't accept the literature after hearing his Hindi, for even though he was trying to be a Rajasthani, he still looked and sounded like an outsider. Often he ended up the day with one meager rupee. Then he went to a roadside eating stand and had a glass of milk and a couple of *samosas* (fried vegetable patties).

There was an old church in the town, built in the days of British colonialism, and Mathews decided to attend services there. Right away he began visiting homes and praying for those in the church who were sick. This caught the attention of the pastor, Daulat Masih. Masih had a real missionary heart, and he had longed for a young man to travel to the villages with him. Mathews had impressed him because he had not seen anyone like him with a heart for the villagers. He encouraged Mathews to go to the villages with him and learn the village customs and culture. "Mathews," he would say, "You are the man I wanted; but you have to learn Hindi better, and you have to learn how to talk to the local people."

For more than two years Pastor Masih gave him lessons in mission work there in the villages of Rajasthan. Through Masih's guidance, Mathews learned not only how to talk to the village people—he learned how to love them as his own.

Chapter Seven

Summer Heat–Winter Chills

Summer Heat

*R*ajasthan, the land that Mathews adopted as his own, had a climate that was far different from the one that produced the rivers, lakes, rainforests, and lush green rice fields of his native Kerala. The Great Thar Desert reached from Pakistan into Rajasthan, giving the region a hot, dry climate, in contrast to the wet, humid weather that the rest of India received. Summer meant dry, unrelenting heat. During this time of year the temperature often soared well above 100º F.

In the heat of summer, water was scarce in this arid environment and became a very precious commodity. Sometimes a couple of villages had to share a well. Because of the heat, the women would cluster around the wells early in the morning or late in the evening with their empty clay pots. Then they would fill them and return to their homes with the heavy pots brimming with water—just like the Samaritan woman in the Bible. Each family owned one or two water pots, which were kept outside on the veranda. Wooden lids covered the pots, and on the lid a brass mug was placed to scoop water out. This water was freely offered to anyone who came to the door.

On one of these hot summer afternoons, Mathews was witnessing in a village, going from house to house. As he stood at the doorstep of one of these dwellings, he spotted a water pot. Being very thirsty, he thought it would be okay to take a drink of water. So he took the mug in his hand, lifted the lid, dipped the mug into the pot, and poured the water into his mouth.[7]

As he was drinking, a man came out of the house and eyed Mathews with the mug in his hand.

"Where are you from?" he gruffly barked.

"Kerala," said Mathews.

"What is your caste?" he questioned.

Mathews replied, "I am a Christian."

Now in India, the caste system is very important to most people, for it places people into different levels of social standing. A person from a lower caste is not supposed to touch the water pot, no matter how thirsty he may be. If a person from a lower caste drinks from the water supply of a higher caste person, he pollutes it, according to religious law. Because Mathews was a Christian, the man of the house considered him "untouchable"—a level even lower than the lowest caste.

Upon learning that Mathews was a Christian, the villager became so incensed that he grabbed the precious water pot, raised it over his head, and heaved it at Mathews. The pot missed its mark, but the fleeing missionary realized as he ran that the spiritual climate in this land was as dry as the desert.

Often, after incidents like this, Mathews would chuckle, thinking about how superstitious many of these village people were. At the same time his heart ached seeing them live in darkness. Jesus was teaching the young evangelist how He feels for the lost: "But when He [Jesus] saw the multitudes, He was moved with compassion for them, because they were weary and scattered, like sheep having no shepherd" (Matthew 9:36).

Winter Chills

The heat in Rajasthan was, at times, unbearable. Summer did eventually give way to winter, but then nighttime desert temperatures plunged to freezing. Mathews tried to keep himself warm on frosty winter nights by lighting his cook stove and sitting in front of it. Then he would turn his back to the stove and warm it up. Only by doing this could he finally get to sleep. In the early morning, when the cold once again crept inside his light clothing, he would relight the kerosene stove.

Mathews was not prepared for the cold, coming from the more temperate southern regions, and his body was not acclimated to the extreme temperature swings. Without proper food and enough warm clothes, he first caught pneumonia, then malaria, and finally hepatitis.

Some of his friends admitted the very sick Mathews to the government hospital in Udaipur. The doctor who examined him prescribed some medicines, which Mathews was instructed to purchase from the medical shop at the hospital and begin taking regularly. But since he didn't have any money, he couldn't buy the medicine. He couldn't even afford to buy milk or fruit to help strengthen himself.

On his fourth day in the hospital, the doctor visited Mathews on his rounds and scolded him when he learned that he had not been taking the medicine. After he left, the nurses, out of pity, secretly collected some money among themselves and put it in an envelope. Then they all gathered around Mathews' bed. The head nurse handed him the envelope and said, "Brother, you need medicine, milk, and fruit. Your body has become very weak. We feel very sorry for you, so here is some money. Get your medicine and some good food; the rest is for your train ticket back to Kerala. You have nobody to help you here. Why should you die in Rajasthan? Go back to your home. Later you can come back when you feel well again."

When she finished speaking, he handed the envelope back. "Dear sister," he muttered weakly, "you should not feel sorry for me. I cannot return to Kerala. I have come here to live or to die. It does not make any difference to me. But thank you for caring. Please take this gift back."

The nurses were shocked, but they complied with his wishes. However, they took the money, bought the medicine for Mathews, and gave *that* to him instead. After ten days he finally began to find some relief from his illness. On his request, the doctor discharged him from the hospital, and he returned to his small room.

Mathew's hospitalization had placed him in contact with that head nurse—Nora Sen, from Delhi—who had presented the money to him. She was the head of all nurses in the Udaipur government hospital. Intrigued by Mathews' testimony, she began to attend his prayer meetings after his recovery. Soon she received Christ as her Savior and was baptized.

Nora greatly influenced the medical staff at the hospital after her conversion. Every Tuesday many of them would come to her government residence, which was a large house located on the hospital premises, for prayer and Bible study. As time went by a number of those nurses received the Lord and joined Mathews' church as well.

Mrs. Sen had a son, Vimal, who was very wild in his youth. A bully and a fighter, he would not go to school, and his mother was always in tears for him. But Mathews took him into his home and loved him as a younger brother. Before long he, too, decided to follow Jesus. Vimal became a great help on Mathews' bicycle tours to the remote areas. In later years, he himself became an evangelist. Then he again accompanied Mathews to the villages, this time to preach and sing. His mother praised God for changing her son's heart.

The sickness and hospitalization of a cold, weary, half-starved young missionary in the hands of a loving, all-knowing

Savior had made all of that possible. Mathews knew that his experience brought on by the cold winter nights was not only for *his* own good: Jesus used it to make Nora Sen, many of the other nurses, and Nora's son channels of blessing as well. Mathews was learning that, whatever happens in the life of God's people, whether good or bad, the Lord always has a purpose for it; and it always contributes to God's glory. As Paul, the apostle, said in Philippians 1:12, "The things which happened to me have actually turned out for the furtherance of the Gospel."

Chapter Eight

Cries of Faith

*G*etting started on a faraway mission field, living among strangers with a different culture and a different language, living by faith in God for his needs; these circumstances provided fertile soil for frequent prayers to an all knowing and loving God—and many answers.

Once again Mathews found himself with no money to pay the rent for his room for three months in a row. Finally the landlord came to him and said, "Tomorrow I will kick you out if you don't give me forty-five rupees (about one dollar). Because you told me that you were a missionary from Kerala, I thought you had enough money; but now I see that you don't. You cheated me. Tomorrow I will come at 10 o'clock in the morning and evict you if the rent is not paid."

The owner used very rude language as he left, and Mathews was shocked. But he thought, *God, I am not insulted. These words are against You, Lord. I am here because You sent me here.*

That night he could not sleep. He opened his Bible to Matthew 6:33: "But seek first the kingdom of God and His righteousness, and all these things shall be added to you."

"God," he pleaded, "You promised 'all these things.' I don't want *all* these things—I just need 45 rupees before tomorrow morning." He placed his finger on the verse in his Bible and began to really cry to God, saying, "God, tomorrow morning, please do a miracle." Then he fell asleep.

At 9 o'clock the next morning he awoke, but he was afraid to go out of the house. He still had no money, but he didn't want to borrow from anyone because he was so new to the area. Not only that, he hadn't eaten for the past couple of days. Then he heard a knock on the door. Mathews thought, *Why has this man come earlier than what he told me last night?*

Hesitantly he opened the door and peered out; but instead of seeing the owner, the postman was standing there. He handed the surprised Mathews a money order for fifty rupees! A Christian woman in Kerala had sent the money ten days earlier. Mathews rejoiced and broke into thanksgiving to the Lord as he closed the door.

At 10 a.m. the owner arrived, right on time, and Mathews was waiting for him. With a smile, he handed him the rent money—all of it. The owner was surprised. "Where did you get this money?" he asked in disbelief. "Did you borrow it from somebody? Did you tell anybody what I told you last night?"

Mathews answered simply, "No. I prayed to my God."

"You prayed to your God last night...and this morning the money came?" He was quiet for a moment; then he said, "Your God is a real God. Your God is an *instant* God. Our gods and goddesses are there, but they don't help. We cry to them for years and they never listen. But you—you pray one night, and you get the money the next morning!"

Then he added, "I am so sorry! I will not come to you anymore for rent. Whenever you get money from your God, you can bring it to my home. I will not ask you anymore."

This lesson from the Lord provided Mathews with one of his first experiences in faith. The Lord Jesus had said, "Ask and you shall receive, that your joy may be full" (John 16:24). Mathews asked, and Mathews received.

One day Mathews was visiting homes in the city and praying for sick people. By the afternoon he had been cycling for a long time, and since he hadn't eaten any breakfast or lunch, he was very hungry. He stopped to pray for one particular sick lady, and as he was leaving, much to his surprise, she gave him an egg wrapped in paper. She said, "Brother Mathews, take this home and boil and eat it. You look so hungry and tired."

He had not mentioned to the lady that he was hungry; he just shared a few things from the Bible and prayed for her. After she gave him the egg, he thanked her and returned home. After thanking the Lord for His provision, he boiled the egg and ate it. Later in his life God provided him with a lot of delicious food, but the egg wrapped in paper that he received that day was tastier, more delicious, and more precious than anything he ever ate. Mathews had enrolled in God's school, and God was teaching him that he would indeed provide for even the little things of his life, one day at a time.

Another lesson was once again provided through hunger and a money order—this one from his parents. His father sent him some money once in a while, even though he still owed money for sending his son to college. Mathews' mother also would occasionally send a little money.

Mathews had gone without food for some time. He was remembering the good old days at home when his mother used to cook delicious food for him and he would eat it all; or the times when he would go to a restaurant in town with his friends and eat whatever he liked. He enjoyed playing soccer, which gave him an excellent appetite. There in the South he ate a lot, but not here in northern India. Here he often went hungry.

On this particular day he had been praying since morning, and he was very hungry. As he prayed, the postman arrived.

Mathews went to the door, and the carrier handed him a money order from his mother for five rupees—about ten cents! That was the smallest money order he ever received, but it came in time to buy a little bit of food. There was a note at the bottom. It read, "Dear son, two of these rupees are mine. I had no money at home, but we had some eggs, and I sold them for two rupees. The other three rupees were a gift from a sister in our church. She gave me the money and said, 'Send this money to your son.' So I am sending these five rupees. Perhaps you may need them for some small thing."

At this time, the small thing Mathews needed most was food! The Lord was mindful to give him what he needed just at the right time, and in this way He took care of his need.

Deliverance from desperate situations came in many different ways. One morning Mathews was distributing tracts in an old part of Udaipur. The shops and houses nestled close to each other, making it a congested, dark area. He had just started witnessing in the houses and to the shopkeepers, and word of his activity quickly got around. Soon a crowd gathered in front of a shop where he was preaching, and some of the people started getting angry. At length one of them shouted, "Why do you want to give us a foreign religion? Go away from here or we will kill you!"

The crowd became so incensed that they began to chase him. Mathews turned and ran away as fast as he could and darted into a dark, narrow alley. A moment later he came upon an old man sitting in the gloom and breathlessly pleaded, "Sir, I have come here from a far-off state just to tell the people here about the Lord Jesus Christ, who saved my life when I was drowning. Some people are chasing me, and they said they would kill me. Please help me!"

At that point the angry crowd caught up with Mathews, but at once the old man stood up and ordered, "Don't chase this young fellow. He's a young man like you. He's by himself, and he is not forcing you to take anything or to purchase anything. He was just giving out some good literature about what he knows. If you don't want it, leave him alone."

This elderly man was an influential figure in that area, so after the young men heard what he had to say, they left.

After pouring out his thanks, Mathews continued down the narrow alley. But the crowd of young men, after walking away from Mathews and the old man, had run down the alley and hidden, waiting for him to come their way. As he passed by, they grabbed him by surprise and dragged him to a grain warehouse with thick stone walls. Throwing him inside, they locked the door from the outside and went away.

Inside the windowless building there was no light, and there was no ventilation. Mathews knew that the young men planned to come back after it was dark outside and beat him; possibly even kill him. He was the first person ever to bring a "foreign god" into their neighborhood, and they were not going to tolerate that.

For a while he sat and pondered the situation. He decided that banging on the door to be heard was useless because it was so thick. The walls were made of stone, so yelling would do no good either. Finally, in desperation he cried out: "God save me from this place!" Even though he didn't have a watch and didn't know exactly how long he had been in there, he knew that it had been hours. He was in a dark dungeon—and it was getting dark outside.

Suddenly the door quietly opened; but it was the kind old man down the alley who entered. He had learned from one of the young men what had happened and where Mathews was being held. He said in a low voice, "Don't stay around here— don't give tracts to anybody. Just go." With a wave of his arm, he continued, "Take this path and get out of this place. Run away, and don't look back." So Mathews followed the old man's advice and ran off quickly into the night.

Once again the Lord had come to his aid just in time. "The eyes of the Lord are on the righteous, and His ears are open to their cry" (Psalm 34:15).

Udaipur had been Mathews' home for more than a year, and though at twenty years of age still very young himself, he was praying to God to give him some young people from that town. He prayed, "Lord, I may not be able to establish a church or accomplish much, but if You give me a handful of North Indian young people, I can tell them about what You have done for me, and I can teach them the Bible and disciple them. Then, they can continue the work better than I would be able to do."

This may seem to be a simple prayer, but in its simplicity an evidence of humility coupled with steadfast faith showed through. Though very young, here was a man God could refine and use.

In the church Mathews attended occasionally, there was a young man named Samson. He and the rest of his family were Christian in name only, and they lived non-Christian lives. The Lord led Samson to Mathews, and when Mathews shared the Gospel with him, he was attracted. Before long Mathews won him to the Lord.

However, Samson's parents soon found out. They had called Mathews, *dubki-wala,* which means "immersion fellow," knowing that he belonged to a group that baptized people by immersion. They told the people, "The immersion fellow has grabbed our son. If we get hold of him, we will break his legs."

Samson did not want to go back to his home, because his family would beat him; so Mathews took Samson into his care. The two lived together, and Mathews used the opportunity to teach Samson truths from the Word.

One winter day Samson decided that the Lord wanted him to be baptized; so Mathews and Samson went by bicycle to a nearby lake. There, in the chilly winter air, Mathews secretly baptized him. His parents didn't learn about their son's baptism until six months later, but by that time Mathews had made friends with them.

Samson was nineteen years old and Mathews only twenty when this took place. He became the first person that Mathews baptized. Samson eventually became a pastor in Jodhpur. (In the future his son would become an evangelist after graduating from the Bible college that Mathews later founded)

Chapter Nine

Mary and Marriage

$\mathcal{M}$ary George was raised in a large, God-fearing farm family in the village of Koottala, in northern Kerala. Her parents were born-again, committed Christians. Mary herself had invited Jesus into her heart when she was quite young, but when she was only ten years old, tragedy struck—her mother died.

Life suddenly became very hard for Mary. She was left with three younger siblings to care for, and her father and her older brothers as well. Every day she did chores on the farm and then caught the bus for school. When she got home each afternoon, all the household chores were waiting.

Sometime during the long weeks and months that followed her mother's death, Mary began to lose her faith in God. One thought continually haunted her: *My father is a godly man. My mother was extremely godly, and we need our mother so much! What sin did any of us commit that God would deal with us so cruelly?*

Mary was so upset that she quit praying. She lost interest in going to church and reading her Bible as well, but for fear of what her father would say she maintained an outward conformity. She especially hated going to prayer meetings because she didn't believe in the manifestations of the Holy Spirit, like her father did. But he, in spite of his deep loss, continued to serve the Lord (and eventually married a godly woman).

One day, just before Mary's tenth-grade final examination, a prophet named Moses came to their village. He was a man of prayer, and during the day he visited homes and led prayer meetings, which were attended by many neighborhood people. At night they met in the village church for revival prayer meetings. The time was spent praying, including prayer for healing and prophesying; there wasn't much preaching. Not surprisingly, feeling the way she did about prayer meetings, Mary did not want to attend.

The daytime prayer meetings were held in homes, and after a few days they met in Mary's house. Mary, however, decided to leave for school early that morning so that she would be gone before Moses came. She also planned to stay after school for awhile so that she could avoid the entire meeting. But God had other plans.

The bus passed through her village every half hour. Mary was waiting at the bus stop promptly at 8:00 a.m., when it usually arrived; but by 10:30 the bus had not yet come. Confused and upset, she started for home.

It troubled Mary as she walked that all those praying people were in her house, and she began to hate them. When she got home, she entered through the back door and quietly dropped into the last line of people sitting on the floor. However, she did not do so unnoticed.

The moment she came into the room, Moses stood up. He looked at her across the crowded room and prophesied: "The Lord says, 'My daughter, you are angry with *Me*. You are so offended by *Me*. I know your heart; you are rebelling against My Spirit. But I want you to understand that I took your mother for a reason. For one mother I will give you thousands and thousands of mothers in North India. Through you I will save thousands of souls. Get prepared, for I have chosen you for *My* ministry.'"

It was like a lightning bolt from the blue. She had never seen this man before, and she knew nothing about North India. But her heart, hardened by anger against God for taking her mother, began to melt. Then the prophet walked over to her, placed his hand on her head, and prayed for her. The moment he finished, Mary was filled with the Holy Spirit and burst into unknown tongues, praising and worshipping God. A Mighty Power overtook her. The moment she was baptized in the Holy Spirit, her whole thinking pattern, her outlook on life, and her attitude toward God all changed; and she experienced God's peace.

Mary easily passed her high school final examination, but now she was faced with a dilemma. Her father wanted her to go to college, but her heart yearned to see the prophecy come true—to minister to the people in northern India.

Mary's ambition was to go to Bible school, but in 1964 women didn't go to Bible school—only men did that. So Mary struggled within. Many people said to her, "You have such good marks; and since you lost your mother, you should go to college. Then you can get a fairly good job, have a decent life, and help your family."

However, she didn't listen to this advice. At sixteen years of age she decided to go to Hebron Bible School in Kumbanad. She studied there for one year and did very well. The principal of the school, Pastor Abraham, told Mary that since she was such a good student, she should go to the Southern Asia Bible Institute, located in the city of Bangalore, in neighboring Karnataka state.

This advice Mary did decide to follow, even though Bangalore was a long way from home. She was granted admission and studied there the next year. The principal's wife, who taught

Mary songs in English while she was a member of the choir, advised her to complete the three-year course there, and she promised to sponsor her for further studies.

Mary was happy that the Lord opened the way for her to get excellent training in an English Bible college, and she didn't regret not going to a secular school. After one year she came back to her home in Kerala for her summer vacation.

United Hearts

Meanwhile, the editor of a new Christian magazine in Kerala came to Udaipur in Rajasthan and interviewed Mathews. By this time Mathews was well known in the Kerala churches because of the drowning incident and his mission to North India. He asked Mathews questions about his drowning experience, his call to the ministry, how he came to Rajasthan, and about his missionary experiences there. The editor then wrote a very stirring article, and he asked Mathews to write an article as well, challenging people to go to North India. Both articles appeared in the same inaugural issue.

When he returned to the South, the editor visited several churches, promoting his new magazine. It just so happened that a copy of that first issue fell into Mary's hands during her vacation time at home. As she read the stories, they kindled in her heart a desire for Rajasthan. Because the articles on the North had challenged her so much, she kept the magazine with her in the bottom of her suitcase.

God was moving in mysterious ways. The people of North India lay in the bondage of sin, but He was orchestrating events in the far-off South to bring light into their darkness.

It is important to remember that in India, as mentioned before, either the parents or a pastor can propose marriage between a Christian man and woman, and either side can initiate the process. But usually the parents, the pastors, and the elders of the family—the grandparents and uncles—are all involved. They get together and talk, and if there is an agreement, those from the young woman's side will go and visit the young man's side, or vice-versa. In those days this meeting marked the first time that the man and woman saw each other.

It was providential that Mathews' mentor from Kerala, Pastor P.M. Philip, knew both Mary and her family and Mathews and his family; and knowing their love for the Lord and their attraction to the North as well, he proposed a marriage between the two.

So Mathews' father, his uncles, and their pastor went to Trichur in Kerala. There they met with Mary's father, P.V. George, her grandmother and other relatives, and Pastor Philip as well. Although they had never met, Mathews had seen Mary's photograph. Even during the first part of the meeting, he couldn't see her. She stayed in the kitchen while the other ladies of the family served coffee, tea, and snacks.

During the meeting the pastors discussed whether Mary and Mathews represented a good match. Then Pastor Philip called to Mary, asking her to bring some water for all of them. Mary, very shy, appeared at the door of the kitchen, blushing and looking down.

Pastor Philip said, "Thomas, you can talk to Mary now."

Mathews, speaking to his future bride for the first time, asked, "Are you willing to come to Rajasthan as a missionary?"

Mary nodded.

Then he asked her a second question. "Are you prepared to leave your studies and come to Rajasthan immediately after the marriage?"

She was silent. For days she had pondered the choice between going to college as her father desired and following the Lord's call to the North, and now she was faced with a monumental decision. Pastor Philip gently insisted, "Please answer."

She softly spoke: "As my father decides."

Then Thomas Mathews spoke one more time. "I have no salary, and I don't own a house. I have a very small church, and we worship in a rented building. There will be many sufferings and hardships. Are you ready to face that with me?"

There was no hesitation. Mary nodded again and quickly disappeared into the kitchen. That was all they said to each other. They were not permitted to talk privately.

When she left the room, everyone turned to Mary's father. Mr. George voiced his agreement with her decision by speaking the words from Genesis 24:50 that Rebekah's father spoke to Abraham's servant: "The thing comes from the Lord."

Pastor Philip stood up and said, "Friends, the matter for which we have come is now finalized. Let us fix a date for the marriage." The wedding date was set for the next month, on June 9, 1966. When they had all prayed together, the meeting was over, and they all ate an excellent meal. Mary even helped in serving.

In Kerala the parents of the bride had to give a dowry to the groom's family, which can represent a lot of money. This often placed a tremendous strain on less affluent families. But Mathews determined not to take any money from Mary's father. He told his parents, "We should not ask anything from Mary's family. She has dedicated her life for mission work just as I have."

Mathews also decided not to burden his own father for any expenses, like buying a new suit. He wanted the preparation costs to be minimal. His father told him that he could borrow some money, but Mathews declined. He felt that such spending would be a waste, and he wanted to be an example of simplicity.

So he didn't buy anything new for the wedding. He wore his old shirt, pants, and shoes. He didn't even purchase so much as a new handkerchief! He washed and ironed his clothes well, doing everything deliberately as an act of consecration to his Lord. Mary was clad in a white sari.

By custom the wedding was held in the bride's church, so Mathews and his family again traveled the 150 miles to Koottala. It was a wonderful ceremony, with hundreds of family members and friends in attendance. That evening the bride and groom traveled back to the home of Mathews' parents in Punalur with those who came in the bridegroom party. The next day all the people from the neighborhood who could not come to the wedding dropped in to meet the new bride.

Chapter Ten

Northward Together

In the days that followed, the newly married couple traveled to different towns in the surrounding area to preach, including the hometown of Pastor P.M. Philip, where Mathews had studied in the Bible school for four months. That was a very dear place to him. During the Sunday service the couple shared their testimonies, and Pastor Philip prayed for them and blessed them.

A few days later they went to meet Pastor K.E. Abraham, since Mary had been his student. It was especially meaningful for Mathews to sit with him at the table. After lunch and visiting for some time, they bowed their heads and Pastor Abraham also prayed for them and blessed them.

As June drew to a close, the day came for the newlyweds to leave for the North Indian mission field. Some of their relatives had given them food to take along, and many of them came to the railway station to wave goodbye. Mathews was twenty-two, and Mary was eighteen.

When they arrived in Udaipur, however, only a few people were at the station to greet them; but the joyful couple headed off to the house Mathews had already rented—a large, eight-room house belonging to the local ruler. It was aptly called *Manohar Bhawan*, which means "beautiful house." When they walked into their new home, they prayed together for God's blessing. During the first three or four days, everyone in the congregation there came to welcome them, and they had wonderful fellowship together.

Their first lesson in faith presented itself rather quickly. Within a few days the food they had brought with them from the South ran out, and they had little money left. However, the church members had no idea they were going hungry. They assumed that since the newlywed couple had just come from their homeland, they would have brought enough money.

The next week they ate only snacks and drank only tea. When they visited homes they would have the same thing—snacks and tea. Sometimes the host would offer Mathews and Mary a meal, but the couple only accepted when they were invited ahead of time. Still, they were joyous and excited, even though their "honeymoon" began with half starvation!

The furnishings in their house were sparse, with no cot or mattress; so they slept on the floor. Shortly after they arrived in Rajasthan, the three-month rainy, humid season came. During this time their bed sheets were soaking wet from the condensation on the floor.

When the first winter arrived, even though they still slept on the floor, they improvised to meet the demands of the cold weather. Taking three or four old cotton bed sheets, Mary stitched them together and made a sort of comforter to help keep them warm. An old kerosene pump-stove, given to Mathews by a friend, was used for cooking.

They inaugurated their ministry together by visiting homes and praying for people, and they led a few souls to Christ. All day they would go from house to house on their bicycle, with Mathews steering and Mary sitting on the back. They pushed themselves, even though they went without food for three or four days a week. Without any luxuries, but thankful because they were together in the service of their King, they firmly believed that God would bless them with many souls.

Mary made vital contributions to the ministry. She was Mathews' mainstay and number one supporter. When they were suffering and facing starvation, she remembered Paul's confidence—"I am exceedingly joyful in all our tribulation" (2 Corinthians 7:4)—and would strengthen her husband saying, "Let us not worry; let us face it with joy!"

Grace From Above

Mathews often left to preach in other states or teach in a Bible college. Mary stayed by herself in that big house in the heart of the city for up to a month at a time. One day, when Mathews returned home after being gone several weeks, Mary confided that she had gone without food for many days. "You and I are both strong and we can suffer like this, half starved" she said, her eyes wet with tears. "But I don't think we should have any children. I can't think about letting our children starve like this. It is better not to have children, because it would be so hard to see our children going without food."

These moving words from the heart of his wife were more than Mathews could bear, because they came from one who had endured months of hunger and suffering. But he encouraged her, saying, "Let us leave it to God. If God wants to give us children, I believe He will provide for them. If He doesn't want to give us a child, that will be okay. We will have spiritual children." So they resigned the dilemma to the hands of the Lord, abandoning it to His sweet will.

Nearly two years after they were married, Mary neared the time when she would deliver their first child. They didn't have any clothes for the new baby, because they had no money. In fact, they still didn't have enough to provide regular meals for themselves.

The day before the baby was born, Mary went into labor. Together she and her husband packed her old clothes and some cloths to wrap around the baby. The hospital was nearby, and Mathews needed only half a rupee to hire a horse cart to take her there; but he didn't have even half a rupee. He felt it wouldn't be wise to take her by the main road since she was in pain and would be noticed. But there was a shortcut from their house to the hospital, and Mathews managed to guide her down that path.

Usually when a mother is admitted for childbirth, she has enough clothes and other necessities for the child. But Mary had only brought the old cloths because that was all they had. That evening the nurse in the ward, who happened to know Mathews, asked him, "Why didn't you bring clothes, soap and powder, and the other things for your baby?"

Mathews felt bad, but there was nothing he could do.

Grace was born the next morning and wrapped in the old cloths. When Mathews came to the hospital to see the baby for the first time, he felt so sorry because he still had not bought anything for her.

The couple returned to their home, bearing God's precious gift. Once in the house, Mathews began to cry before the Lord because of their needs. But when he remembered that Jesus was wrapped in swaddling clothes and laid in a manger as a baby, the Lord gave him peace.

Three days later a money order from a friend arrived. With overflowing joy and deep gratitude, he bought everything that the mother and child needed. In addition, a few church members brought gifts for the newborn baby.

Believing and Rejoicing

In l969 the monthly rent for Manohar Bhawan was raised from 125 to 150 rupees. The Udaipur church was still in the infant stage, and the monthly offering only averaged forty-five rupees. Occasional unexpected gifts came in times of extreme need. Whatever money Mathews and Mary received was first applied to the house rent. With the leftover amount, other needs like food were taken care of.

Their second daughter, Glory, was born in 1971, and son Paul in 1974. In those days of hardship, God's promise, "My righteous one will live by faith," (Hebrews 10:38 NIV), gave courage to the family.

Life in the winter was very hard at times. The temperature would sometimes get as low as 32 degrees. They didn't have a cot to sleep on, and they had no quilt.

However, Pastor P.M. Philip from Kerala, after staying for some time in Delhi, came to Udaipur for a visit on his way back home. Before he left the Mathews', he surprised them. He said, "I am returning to Kerala, and since I won't need my quilt there, I am leaving it with you." It was a double quilt, and it was the first and only one that the family had for another five years.

On another occasion, a sister in their church, Miss Olive, brought them a surprise gift—a cot! Both the parents and the children were sleeping on the floor on sheets prior to that. But they were happy nonetheless because they knew that they were sacrificing for the sake of the Gospel. Mathews and Mary used these practical, everyday situations to teach their children that if they suffered patiently and willingly for the Lord, then God would bless them. The children gladly accepted this instruction because they saw these principles lived out by their parents.

The Mathews' often survived with a bare minimum of food and other needs, since hardly any money was ever left after paying the rent. But a month came when they had no money on the tenth—the due date. Mathews asked and received permission from the owner to pay it on the fifteenth.

And once again God did not fail them. On the fifteenth, a money order for 250 rupees arrived. As the postman handed over the money order to sign, both Mathews and Mary were overcome with joy and began shouting "Hallelujah!" lifting up their hands and praising God.

Unfortunately, they were so full of joy and gratitude that they forgot to take down the name and address of the donor. They contacted the post office later, but to no avail. They were very sad that they could not write a letter of thanks to the generous person whom God used to send the money at the right time.

Early one morning, Grace woke up and began to cry, asking for an apple. They didn't have any apples, because apples were expensive and there was no money. Mary tried every way of consoling the little girl, but she would not listen. Both the mother and father were deeply moved by her unusual and continuous weeping.

Later Mary began to sweep the room where some guests had spent the previous night. As she was sweeping under the cot, her broom touched something. Mary bent down and peered under the cot, and to her amazement she found two apples that the guests had left behind! Baby Grace had cried for one apple, but instead of one she got two. How caring God was to the cries of their child.

During those times of deprivation, Mary's older brother came from Kerala to visit the family. He arrived without any notice, while Mathews was away in another state traveling and preaching. No one from Mary's family had ever visited her in North India since her marriage. Of course Mary was very happy, but she was apprehensive as well. There was no food in the home, and there wasn't any money either. However, she made tea, and she and her brother had a good visit. Then he went to take a shower and wash his clothes.

Mary sat down on the floor at the entrance of Manohar Bhawan, holding Glory in her lap, and began to weep. She prayed for just a few rupees to buy some rice to serve her brother. When she opened her eyes, wonder of wonders!—they fell upon something shiny lying in the sand in the courtyard. Scrambling to her feet, she ran to the object and picked it up; it was a one-rupee coin. She couldn't believe her eyes! Then she discovered that her foot had uncovered another coin...and then another. Altogether she found five coins.

Mary knew the coins belonged to someone who had dropped them, and she knew the Lord wanted her to find their owner. Since there were no other houses nearby, she went to a nearby shop and asked if anyone had lost any coins. When she heard the negative reply, she ran to the rice shop nearby, praising the Lord all the way, and bought a kilogram of rice (about two pounds), some vegetables, and milk and sugar with those five rupees.

By the time her brother finished with his shower and laundering, Mary had spread a wonderful lunch on the table, and they ate and talked. He never realized how the Lord had provided the money for that meal. Later he went with her to the grocery store and bought all the things needed in the kitchen for the rest of his stay.

On another occasion when Mathews was again away preaching, a guest came to the house for a few hours. Mary did have something to offer for lunch this time, but she did not check the stove to see if it had any kerosene. Rice and vegetables were placed on the stove to cook, but before they were half done the kerosene in the stove ran out. The flame began to flicker, and she knew that she had no money to buy a bottle of kerosene, even though it would cost only half a rupee.

With great faith she pumped the stove anyway and praised the Lord saying, "Thank you Jesus! Thank you Jesus!" The flame picked up and the water began to boil. After a few minutes the flame started dying once more. But in faith she resumed pumping and praising the Lord, because she knew she couldn't serve her guest half-cooked rice. Then again the flame leaped up and wonderfully burned for some time. After three or four such demonstrations of faith the rice was well cooked, and she served it with a grateful heart.

School Struggles

Several years later, Mathews and Mary sent Grace and her younger sister, Glory, to the local convent school. It was the only girls' school in Udaipur where classes were taught in English; the other schools spoke only Hindi. Most of the children there were from rich upper-class families. The two Mathews girls were a contrast, perhaps the poorest children in the school. Often they sat under a tree without any food at lunchtime, while all their friends took their lunch boxes and gathered together in groups of three or four to eat.

Sometimes there wouldn't be any food at home either. Their mother would tell them, "Girls, go ahead to school. If God gives us any money, I will bring lunch for you."

On such occasions Grace and Glory went to school, and then at lunchtime they ran to the gate and stared down the road to see if their mom was coming. Some days she didn't come; then they would go to the water tap, drink water deeply, and return to the shade of the tree and wait for the class bell. Once in a while the school maid, Ruth, who knew Grace and Glory very well, shared her lunch with them.

The children saw many days of extreme need, but one day a package arrived. It came from a sister in the U.S.A. named Alice Shevkenek, who had met the Mathews family on a visit to Udaipur in the past. The parcel was eagerly opened, and they found brand new clothes for both the girls inside. Tears of gratitude rolled down Mary's cheeks as she examined the contents. God once again proved Himself trustworthy and faithful.

On several occasions Grace was turned away from school because Mathews could not pay the monthly tuition on time. When this happened she would be told to stand up and leave. "Take your bag and walk; no more bus either," the teacher once told her. That time Grace stayed home from school for five days and cried. Mathews and Mary prayed at these times, and God always provided help through someone—on several occasions someone quite unknown. Then they sent her back to school.

Grace, being the oldest child, suffered more than the other two children because as time went by, the Mathews' had more support from their church. Many times she had no milk to drink and no hot food to eat. Her school uniform, a blue skirt and a white blouse, had become very old. The skirt was so faded that the color turned gray.

One day the teacher told her, "Tomorrow, come with a new uniform or else don't come at all." But they were too poor to get her a new outfit. So she went back to school the next day and hoped that the teacher wouldn't remember. However, when the teacher saw her, she tore the skirt so that Grace couldn't wear it anymore.

Grace borrowed a pin from another student, pinned up her skirt, and walked home crying. When she reached home in tears her parents said, "Don't worry daughter, our God will take care of us. God will provide what we need."

That same afternoon a girl who was in Grace's school ran home and told her mother what had happened at school. This woman was a sister in the Lord who attended the Mathews' church. A little later she brought over one of her daughter's outfits so that Grace could continue going to school.

At times Mathews and Mary went hungry, and their children had hard times as well, but they never regretted it. They often told the children, "Don't worry. If we sacrifice in this way we can establish the Lord's work even in your school." And God honored that faith. When Grace finished high school she was an excellent student and admired by almost everyone in the school.

Experiences at school built character in the Mathews children, and there were surprises as well that taught them that the love of the Lord can come in unexpected ways.

Christmas time often produces wonderful stories of love, and that is as true in Rajasthan as it is anywhere else.

One Christmas Day, after Grace graduated, a van appeared in front of the Mathews' house. Several teachers from the school got out and walked to the door—including the one who tore Grace's dress.

After they were invited in, they explained their mission. It seems that somehow they had recently learned about the trying times the Mathews family had faced during those years when the girls were both in school. One of the teachers apologized, saying, "We never knew that you didn't have a salary and that you were undergoing such sufferings. If we had known, we would have never treated your daughter like that. We are very sorry."

Then the repentant instructors led everyone out to their van. When they opened the doors, the family saw that it was full of new clothes and shoes, and cakes as well—Christmas gifts for the children in the children's home that the Mathews' church had started. Before the women left they asked Pastor Mathews to pray for them, which he gladly did.

Joy to the world! Glory to God in the highest!

Chapter Eleven

In Perils of the Gentiles

*T*he North would not come without a battle. Already Mathews and his family had experienced the trials and perils of hunger and poverty that Paul the apostle came to know so well. In addition, Paul also said in 2 Timothy 3:12, "All who desire to live godly in Christ Jesus will suffer persecution." At first glance, not much consolation is found in these words, especially if one misses meals with regularity. However, Jesus said to *rejoice* when we are persecuted because we would be blessed—*happy*—and we would get heaven as our reward! Mathews was to receive many such "opportunities" to rejoice.

In the 1970's Mathews' church hosted a preaching campaign in Udaipur. A huge crowd came to hear the Gospel, some even coming in bullock carts from far away. Many people were saved, and sick people who were laid on the ground were healed. However, some enemies of the Gospel came up with a plan to disrupt the Lord's work. Several militant Hindus falsely complained to the police that the preaching on the public address system was disturbing the studies of students. However, in reality they weren't really being bothered.

A police official then telephoned Mathews and told him to stop the rally. Mathews explained that permission to hold the meetings for a week had been granted by the authorities. So they were left alone for the time being. But on the fourth day the police appeared at the rally. They arrested Mathews and kept him under police custody the whole night.

When questioned, Mathews repeated what he had earlier stated, "We did the right thing. We had permission."

The authorities responded that the people didn't like to be disturbed. The next morning he was taken to the court and appeared before the judge. However, he only fined Mathews twenty-five rupees, even though it could have been as high as 2,000 rupees. Then he released him on the condition that he never cause a disturbance again. Afterwards, the believers rejoiced at the mercy of their Savior.

A similar incident occurred in the village of Kevdiya. Through Mathews' witnessing in the village in previous years, many people had come to know Jesus and had been baptized. Now two believing couples were getting married, and he was invited to return and conduct the ceremonies. Their relatives, however, became very angry when the young men and women accepted Christ, and they were determined to stop the marriages.

The wedding day arrived. When Mathews entered the village, the relatives and others grabbed him and dragged him in a big procession—jeering, mocking, and kicking him as they went—to the police station, fifteen miles away. The complaint filed against Mathews stated that if he performed the marriages there would be rioting and bloodshed in the village, and that he would be held responsible. Nothing was mentioned about the rioting and bloodshed that had already taken place on the way to the jail.

Late that night he was brought before the district superintendent of police, who was a Muslim. Many of his accusers were also present. The official asked him about his occupation, and Mathews told him he was a priest. As he inquired further, Mathews explained that he held a valid government license to conduct Christian marriages, and then he described what had happened to him. The superintendent looked at Mathews and folded his hands in respect, which was a good sign. Then, since Mathews had been standing the whole time, he asked him to take a chair. So Mathews sat down.

The official said, "Tell me the whole situation as it now stands."

Mathews replied, "The baraats (marriage parties of the bridegrooms) have come, the guests have arrived; and now the brides' people are weeping because the marriages are being cancelled."

When he heard this, the official became enraged. He stood up, taking a big stick in his hand, and began to shout abuse at those who had dragged Mathews there. After threatening to beat them, he chased them out. Then he called for two policemen and instructed them to take Mathews back to the village for the weddings early the next morning.

At 9:00 a.m. the next day, with the police in attendance, the marriages were performed right on time. The people who created the commotion were shamed. And, best of all, most of the people in that village soon turned to Jesus and joined the church that Mathews had started there.

Something else came out of that incident that blessed Christ's Kingdom. A few months later Kamal Masih, the same man who had led the procession carrying Mathews to the police station, paid a visit to Mathews in Udaipur. He said, "I want you to baptize me." God spoke to his heart after the wedding, and he had invited Jesus to be his Savior and Lord. Later he became an evangelist with Native Missionary Movement, and God is still using him in a remarkable way to establish churches.

No, Satan was not about to allow the light of Jesus Christ to penetrate northern India unchallenged. In 1977, the battlefield moved to the national level. That year a government came to power that introduced a bill banning conversion to Christianity. The new political powers also influenced Parliament to introduce a bill to stop the flow of foreign money to Christian organizations in India. For the first time in a heretofore-democratic India, the sky began to become overcast with dark clouds for the Christian minority. A large-scale persecution was brewing.

Christians became united in public protests and private prayer. God moved in the affairs of the nation, and the government was toppled in only two and one-half years, long before it's term ended. In 1980 Mrs. Indira Gandhi and her party came back to power, and Christians breathed a sigh of relief. But the opposing forces in the country slowly continued gaining strength, and incidents of violence began to increase.

PART TWO:

A MOVEMENT

Chapter Twelve

The Beginnings of a Movement

$\mathcal{B}$y 1979 Mathews had started ten churches through the leading of the Lord. Relying on the pattern he learned in his early years, he would get up early in the morning, pack up some chapatis and bundles of Gospel packets on his bicycle, and pedal from village to village. He would be gone the whole day and wouldn't return till late in the evening. In this way he, along with his early co-workers including K.V. Abraham, Samson Wilson, and young believers from his church in Udaipur, covered hundreds of villages.

The villagers were virtually all Hindus in this region, and there were no Christians. In most of the villages, no one had ever even heard the name of Jesus before. In one such village named Pai, eighteen miles from Udaipur, there was a couple named Manohar and Champa. They had been married for ten years, but had no children. One day Champa was admitted to the hospital in Udaipur because she had a large tumor in her abdomen. They were worried because they had no money for the needed surgery. Someone told them, "Go to Thomas Mathews and have him pray for you."

Manohar found Mathews and presented his request. Mathews gladly accompanied him to the hospital, and he talked to the couple about Jesus and how God could bless them if they prayed for Champa. So they did. Soon, she began getting relief from her pain, and the tumor disappeared; then she was discharged from the hospital.

But God had only begun to bless Manohar and Champa. A year later God gave them a son. Mathews dedicated him and called his name Samuel. Samuel later became a full-time evangelist in Rajasthan. After some years they had a second son, Daniel.

Through these miracles, thirty-four people in the village of Pai came to the Lord. Mathews baptized all of them together. Today there is a large church there, and there are thousands of believers in more than thirty other branch churches around Pai, along with a children's home and a school that owe their beginnings to the Pai believers. The Pai church was the first church that was started in the villages of North India.

Twelve miles away from Pai there was another village called Makdadeo, which Mathews rode to on his bicycle. There, after preaching the Gospel and praying for the sick, many gave their lives to Jesus, and soon a local fellowship was started there as well.

Moving Out

In December of 1980 the pastor of the church in Pai, Tajendra Masih, asked Mathews to come there and pray with him for the upcoming new year. "God will tell us something about the coming year," he said. So Mathews went to Pai and spent a few days with Tajendra in prayer. During that time the Lord impressed upon their hearts these words spoken by Jesus: "See, I have set before you an open door, and no one can shut it" (Revelation 3:8).

As they prayed, the Lord showed Mathews a map of India and directed his attention to a certain region that overlapped the states of Maharashtra and Gujarat. The Lord then told him to go there with the Good News. Afterwards, Mathews shared his vision with Tajendra, and they both received it in faith.

Though Mathews had never started any work outside of Rajasthan before, he obeyed God's call. A few weeks later in January of 1981, Mathews, together with Tajendra and three other brothers, headed out to the land of his vision.

With only four hundred rupees and a map of the region, the five of them first traveled south on this journey of faith to Surat in coastal Gujarat, fairly green with vegetation. From there they took a turn west into the interior toward Maharashtra and began a steep ascent into treeless wilderness. Gradually the road vanished as the route climbed up amazingly steep, stony surfaces. Finally, three or four days later, they came to the village of Raniamba on the border between the two states.

Even by Indian standards, Raniamba is remote—an unlikely place for God to begin a movement. They stopped there because Mathews had heard that a large-scale spiritual revival was taking place in that region, and he thought that might have been why God had sent them on their mission.

When they entered the small village, they saw dwellings coated with a rich brown earth-based plaster. They stopped at a house and were invited in. While going through the door, Mathews heard the Lord say to him, "Stay in this house if they receive you. Stay here, and don't wander around"; words similar to the ones in Luke 10:5–9 that Jesus gave the seventy before sending them out.

Gorgi, the homeowner, welcomed them and said to Mathews, "We had a vision that five people would come from Rajasthan, and that we should receive them. We don't even know where Rajasthan is. Are you from there?"

Mathews replied, "Yes, we are."

Gorgi looked at the travelers and was silent for a moment. Then he began to count aloud: "One, two, three, four...five! Oh, *you* are the people the Lord told us about!" He then welcomed each visitor with a big hug.

The visitors from Rajasthan stayed at Gorgi's for two weeks, sharing the Good News of Jesus each day throughout the village and praying for the sick. Every evening they held open meetings. During that time, around two hundred souls committed their lives to Jesus Christ, and they were all baptized.

These new brothers and sisters in Christ were so overjoyed, that when Mathews and his friends felt it was time to depart, they didn't want them to leave. They said, "We need you. God sent you to us, and you should not go back."

Mathews gently explained, "Our families didn't know exactly where we were going, and we haven't written any letters to them. We will go home and tell our wives that we are okay, and then we'll come back."

So the group went back to Udaipur rejoicing. But, in keeping with the promise, they soon returned. They continued traveling and preaching the Word in Raniamba and the surrounding villages for another month, and before long another two hundred people were saved. Within one year, almost five hundred people in that region received Christ and were baptized.

Mathews and Tajendra Masih responded to the Lord's command and went to a new land. A corner was thus turned on what would prove to be the road to an unprecedented movement of the Spirit in the North.

Signs of Hope

Many powerful miracles occurred during these early years to authenticate the moving of God's Spirit among the people of North India. On one occasion Mathews was preaching in a village at an open meeting. While he was speaking, a crowd of people came into view, and they were running toward him. As they drew nearer, Mathews could make out a woman carrying a child that appeared to be dead because it was yellow and pale. The little boy, about four years old, had fallen into a pond and had drowned, and his body had not been found for several hours. The mourners had heard that people were praying in the name of Jesus in the village, and so the crowd ran with the mother and child to the meeting with great hope.

The mother moved through the parted crowd to where Mathews was standing and laid the child in his arms. Mathews was dumbfounded; he had never experienced anything like this before. The child was cold, having been dead for such a long time.

After a moment Mathews told everyone to stand up, close their eyes, and lift their hands to the Lord. He then instructed them to pray for the child, and so they cried to the Lord in earnest. This had been going on for ten or fifteen minutes when the child, almost imperceptibly at first, began moving his arms and legs. Shouting and praising God, Mathews put the little boy on the floor, and he stood up. The people clapped their hands, and they thanked Jesus for the tremendous miracle.

Because of that sign, a big door was opened into the whole region. In the following years, several other incidents of God bringing life to the dead took place through evangelists of NMM.

Another time, a village meeting was being held in the evening. During the meeting several people in a bullock cart drove right into the midst of the crowd. The cart carried a blanket-covered man who was dying of an unidentified disease. He had been sick for many days, and he could not get up. Mathews, who had been preaching, asked what had happened. One of them shouted out, "Pray to your God, and if He is the true God, this man will get up now. If He cannot do that, we will not let you preach in this area—we will kick you out."

It was a very trying situation. Mathews knew that in such a situation he had to throw himself before God. Without speaking he began praying fervently: *God, You have to do it or we are finished!* Then while he was still praying, the sick man stood up in the cart with his blanket in one hand and a stick in the other. He threw the stick away and jumped down to the ground from the cart exclaiming, "I am healed!"

The next morning the same people came back to Mathews and said, "You have to come with us to our village and preach this same God there, too." The whole group along with Mathews walked behind the cart for many miles, and they finally reached the village that evening. They had meetings for two or three days there. Wherever they went people repented of their sins and accepted Jesus, and the sick were healed.

Many other wonderful things took place in Gujarat and Maharashtra, and God opened new doors continually. Mathews had never thought that he would leave Rajasthan; he just wanted to have a church in Udaipur. But God had told him after his drowning experience that He would use him to turn thousands of gentiles to the Living God. And through the loosely organized effort of a few meek and humble supporters of the Gospel under the leadership of the Spirit of Christ, that was beginning to happen.

Chapter Thirteen

Kingdom Women

*The Lord gives the word [of power]; the women who bear
and publish [the news] are a great host*
(Psalm 68:11 Amplified Bible).

*F*or centuries, women in India have been second-class
citizens. Up until recent times they were denied education, and
in many instances they were forced to live a life of slavery. Even
today, when a baby girl is born in a remote village, she is usually
unwanted and rejected. Since the advent of sonography, if the
fetus is found to be a girl, it is often aborted without any
hesitation.

In the sixties and seventies the situation for Christian
women was no different. In fact conditions were more severe
in North India for believing women than for those in the South.
Mary Mathews, however, had had the rare privilege of receiving
Bible training. Consequently, it became her special burden to
work for the Christian women of the North—first for the women
of Rajasthan, and later on, those of the other states. She was
spurred on by the prophecy given her in her younger years: "For
one mother I will give you thousands and thousands of mothers
in North India. Through you I will save thousands of souls."

Thomas Mathews had a very clear stand regarding a woman's role in the church. He was perhaps the first leader in North India to start a women's summer Bible institute, which, together with Mary, he conducted each summer from 1970 to 1982. Young women from many states came to study in the institute. God sent pastors from all over India and some from abroad to minister to the women.

Mathews believed that God had prepared Mary specifically to encourage the women of North India and to serve them in all things. It is significant that many of the regions opened to the Gospel by NMM were actually first touched by Mary and her team. One such example took place in Navapur, Maharashtra.

After the successful opening of Raniamba to Christ in 1981, Mary Mathews and Miss Massey, an elderly Christian lady from Udaipur, visited that village and conducted some meetings. After a week in the area, they traveled to Navapur and several surrounding villages.

In the first new village they entered, they found the central open area where the village elders gathered for discussions, and where marriages and other ceremonies were held—just like the villages in Bible times. They sat under a tree or under a raised platform, and a few women began gathering around them out of curiosity. Mary and her companions asked for some water to drink, in the same way that Jesus did at the well in Samaria, which the village women gladly brought. Then they started a conversation, and later on sang a Hindi devotional song. Then more women, along with many children, came to hear them. The evangelists shared stories from the Gospels, and they told of how the Lord Jesus gave them peace, joy, and healing in their families.

Sadly, it must be mentioned here that many of the village men spend their time brewing liquor to drink and sell, so the burden of providing for the family falls on the women. In many families, they are the ones who must till the farms and take care of the children and the cattle. The women do the shopping at the distant town. Late at night the husband returns home drunk and beats his wife and children.

To these women, family life is a virtual hell. It is not surprising that when they see the joy on the faces of the visitors and hear their stories and songs, they open their hearts and their homes to them, like Lydia did for Paul and his friends in the Book of Acts. If the women of the family in a village are won, the whole village can be led to Jesus. For after the women receive Christ, they can win their children for the Lord. And when at last the men see the change in their families and turn to Jesus, the entire village is Christian.

As the sun was setting that day, one of the village women invited the guests to spend the night in her home. Food was served with love to the guests, and they slept peacefully. Early the next morning some of the women told them about people in the village who were sick, and they led Mary and her friends to their houses. Simple witnessing and prayer followed. Some of the sick got well, but whether they got well or not, those homes were opened for them to return. The following evening many of the men joined the women and children for a Gospel meeting.

This was the ladies' pattern wherever they went, village after village. With more than 500,000 villages in the North, there was always another one tomorrow! In time, Mathews or others would come to these same villages to preach and teach, and eventually a church would be started. In this way, the women's tireless efforts of love paved the way for the beginning of a local church.

Mary also taught the village women principles of modesty. In those early days the women of the interior villages of that area, young and old, wore long saris wrapped around their bodies, with one end of the sari covering the head. They wore no other garment. The village women came to the meetings in large numbers, and young nursing mothers would sit innocently in the front row and breastfeed their babies while preaching was in full swing.

Following one such meeting, Mathews sent Mary a letter, asking her to come to the village where he was preaching with some blouses and saris. A week later Mary arrived and went to work, teaching some of the young ladies to wear saris and blouses together. After three or four years all the sisters in that area picked up the sari-and-blouse style and were dressing modestly.

Chapter Fourteen

Manohar Bhawan

*O*ne day as Mathews witnessed door to door in Udaipur, he met a young man named Philip Thayil. Thayil had developed a serious eye illness, so serious that doctors thought the eye should be removed to halt the spread of infection. He had gone to the best eye hospital in North India, which was located there in Udaipur, but his problem became worse.

Shortly after their meeting, he began to suffer unbearable pain and returned to the hospital. During this time P. M. Philip, Mathews' mentor, visited Udaipur for special meetings. Mathews and Pastor Philip visited Thayil in the hospital, and there in his room they knelt down on the floor by his bed and prayed for him as they touched the green bandage on his eye. As they prayed he was instantly healed. The pain left, and he slept well for the first time in several months. In a short time he was discharged from the hospital.

As a result of being healed, Thayil's life became totally transformed. He began to attend Mathews' church in Udaipur, and became active in evangelism with Mathews. But soon after, he got a job across the Arabian Sea in the country of Oman.

Philip Thayil's healing represented not only an outstanding miracle from God in itself, but as time would show, it also served as a significant turning point in Mathews' ministry. He invited Mathews several times to visit Oman and speak in their meetings. However, Mathews didn't have any interest to go abroad at that time.

Mathews and Mary had lived in the two-story house called Manohar Bhawan for sixteen years, and by 1978 they had three children and a church. One day the ruler who had been renting the place to Mathews sold the property to a businessman. The new owner was an alcoholic, and he had no respect for Mathews' beliefs or his work. When the businessman realized that the rent Mathews was paying was only a fraction of its worth, he decided to sell portions of this big mansion and evict the couple.

When she heard the news, Mary began to weep. She cried out to God, saying, "How can we leave this house? Oh God, do not turn us out of this building." But the man who bought the building was very rich and very hardhearted. Mathews could not bargain with him: they had to leave. Mathews did find a small house to rent. The rent was higher than the big house they were forced to leave, but they had to move. So, they packed and moved most of their belongings, leaving only their bed and a few necessary items to spend their last night.

On their last day in Manohar Bhawan, Mathews called a prayer meeting for that evening and invited all the believers to come. They had planned to move the remaining items to the new house the next morning. While they were worshipping God that night, the Lord gave Mathews a *rhema*—a promise. It was a word of encouragement from Isaiah 52:12, fitting for that exact moment. "You shall not go out with haste, nor go by flight; for the Lord will go before you, and the God of Israel will be your rear guard."

Mathews read this promise to the people and said, "Brothers and sisters, God has given me this verse as a promise. I do not know what will happen, but I believe it will be something extraordinary. Let us take this promise, praise God for it, and let us stand on this promise."

They all praised and thanked God for the promise, but they didn't know what to do about the next morning. After the prayer meeting they were served snacks and tea. Then as they were leaving he said to the young men, "Guys, come tomorrow morning before the shops open at nine and help me put everything in a cart, and we will finish moving out."

They replied, "Yes pastor. We'll be here at six, don't worry." Then they left, and the Mathews family retired for what they supposed would be their last night in Manohar Bhawan.

Around midnight, in the midst of heavy rainfall, they awoke to loud knocking. Mathews shuffled to the door and called out, "Who is there?"

The slurred voice of a man shouted, "Come out! Come out! I have something important to say to you." It was the businessman who had bought the building they were about to vacate. He was drunk.

Mathews replied, "It's midnight. Tomorrow morning at eight, I will hand over the keys to you. Please let us sleep peacefully tonight."

"No, no, no!" he insisted. "I say, come out you fellow!"

Mathews cautiously opened the door and was surprised to see both the businessman and his wife standing there, drenched, in the rain. He urged them to come inside, but the businessman declined. "I don't want to come inside your church," he said, " because I am drunk. I have to tell you something important, but if I tell it, you won't believe me. That is why I brought my wife along." The drunken landlord then turned to his wife and yelled at her to speak out.

His wife complied and said, "My husband, as usual, went to sleep at 10:30 this evening. Around 11:00 he developed a very intense pain in his heart and took all of his pills, but the pain did not subside. So he began to do some poojas.[8] During the pooja, Bhagwan[9] told him, 'Your pain will be relieved if you go to that Christian priest right now and ask him not to vacate the building. Tell him instead to purchase the building and make the payment by the end of December.' Therefore my husband woke me up and asked me to accompany him here to tell you this. Now you may sleep peacefully. You can have this building for your church forever, and you can pay us little by little before the year ends."

Then the man and woman turned and walked to their car to leave. Mathews was dumbfounded. It was too wonderful to believe. But a sudden thought flashed into his mind. Perhaps the drunken owner might change his mind tomorrow and drag him to the court because he broke his word to vacate the building.

He ran after them to the car in the pouring rain and shouted out, "Sir, which Bhagwan told you this?"

The owner exclaimed, "You ask *me* which Bhagwan? What do you mean? Your Jesus Bhagwan alone has told me these things. Who else would tell me such a thing? Be at peace. You can go and sleep—and don't come to me with the key tomorrow!"

Early the next morning Mathews went to the believers who were going to help and said, "Don't come to move the things out. The house is now ours!"

The owner had told Mathews to purchase the building for 60,000 rupees. But although Mathews didn't have the money, he knew that God would provide before the deadline. And God did work another miracle to provide the needed funds.

Soon, Mathews wrote an article about this wonderful experience for the Cross and Crown magazine (see Chapter 17). Across the gulf in Oman, Philip Thayil, the brother who was healed of the eye problem, read the article, and it touched his heart. Motivated by God to contact Mathews, he wrote, "Brother, I have invited you several times to visit, but you have never accepted my invitation. If you want to come at this time, please do so. The money you need can be raised from here. If you don't want to come, don't come; I will not ask you any more."

After reading Thayil's letter, Mathews agreed to come. Thayil sent Mathews the necessary visa papers, some money, and a ticket. Mathews flew across the Arabian Sea to Oman and shared with believers there what God was doing in North India. As a result, enough money was raised to pay off the house before the end of the year. There was even enough money left over to buy a scooter for Mathews, to ease his burden a little. That was the first of many foreign trips in Mathews' life. The Mathews family would leave Manohar Bhawan someday, but not "in haste" or "in flight." God certainly makes things work together for good!

Chapter Fifteen

Filadelfia Bible College

In 1981 Mathews was again invited to Muscat, in Oman, to preach. After giving his testimony in one of the meetings, a man named Thampy Mathews, also a native of Kerala, invited Mathews for a visit. Mathews accepted, and as they shared together in Thampy Mathews' home, Thampy said to him, "Pastor, the Lord wants me to ask you a question. Are you willing to receive a small amount every month so that you can take five North Indian young people and start a small Bible school?"

Mathews answered excitedly, "Yes I am! In fact, I was praying for just that thing."

Thampy handed Mathews five hundred rupees[10] and said, "This is for wheat flour for the students. I can send you this amount every month. Trust God for the rest of the needs."

They prayed over the money before Mathews left, and then he returned to Udaipur. Mathews carefully recruited five promising students from the new village churches and began to train them. Brother Thampy, true to his word, sent five hundred rupees every month. After one year he increased his gift to seven hundred fifty rupees monthly, and then Mathews was able to take on a few more students. Not many months later he upped the amount to one thousand rupees per month, so Mathews once again added more students.

One day Mathews received another letter from Thampy Mathews. "God gave me a very big promotion, and my wife also got a good job," he wrote. "Now we can take on even more students." Enclosed was a money order for 2,500 rupees! This was enough for Mathews to take on twenty or more students. Later Thampy Mathews moved to America, but he collected gifts from his friends in his new homeland and continued to support the college.

From one man's willingness to act on the Lord's prompting, an education in the deeper things of Christ was provided to the people of North India that was destined to have far-reaching consequences. That was how Filadelfia Bible Institute was born.

Mathews continued his relationship with the Indian Christians living in Muscat, traveling there many more times because the believers there appreciated his ministry and his sincerity. They recognized that he loved North Indians, lived among them, and trained and led them. As Mathews took on more students and trained them, he placed them in new areas of ministry, and wherever they went churches were established. In this way the work picked up momentum.

Learning for Jesus

God had called Mathews through his near-drowning experience, and Mathews responded. It took a drastic measure to bring Mathews to the realization that God had greater things in store for him at that time. But his "Here am I! Send me" (Isaiah 6:8) was sincere, like Isaiah's, to the point that he forsook completing his college education and moved to the unknown regions of northern India to share the love of Jesus.

Several years later, however, God began impressing on Mathews that He wanted him to return to school, now that his motives were pure. With a higher degree, Hindus in key places might be more accepting of his purpose, and doors to further spreading of the Gospel might be opened as a result.

Through the urging and support of Philip Thayil, he returned to college and received first his B.A., then his Masters, and finally his Ph.D. degrees. When Mathews, in his high school years, had prepared for his final exam, he had no money to pay the twenty-five rupees necessary to take it. A kind man had offered him the needed money if he would deliver newspapers for three months. Now, during his later college years, the Lord brought in twenty-five *thousand* rupees through fellowships to pay for his expenses.

Mathews remembered the words of the Lord Jesus from Mark 10:29-30: "There is no one who has left house or brothers or sisters or father or mother or wife or children or lands, for My sake and the Gospel's, who shall not receive a hundred-fold now in this time—houses and brothers and sisters and mothers and children and lands, with persecutions—and in the age to come, eternal life."

One hundred fold is not one hundred percent—*one* fold is one hundred percent. One hundred fold is ten *thousand* percent. Jesus offers us a ten thousand percent return in this life in spiritual blessings if we give up everything for Him. For twenty-five rupees Mathews delivered newspapers house to house, but when he gave his life to the Lord's ministry, the Lord blessed him with 25,000 rupees (and much more, later in his life).

With those 25,000 rupees Mathews glorified Jesus even more as the years went by, instead of spending it on himself. This resulted in more money, which also was invested in heavenly treasure. As a result, thousands upon thousands became "mothers" and "brothers" to him when they accepted the Gospel message of eternal life in Christ. Their homes became his homes. The strange northern lands became his lands.

Mathews wrote his Ph.D. dissertation on John Milton, the English poet. Its title was "Divine Providence in 'Paradise Lost' and 'Paradise Regained.'" It was about the "grand design" of God from eternity past to eternity future as revealed in those classic works. As Mathews yielded his life to the will of the Lord, the "Grand Architect" was using him to reveal that design, so that many in North India and beyond could be a part of the eternal paradise that Jesus had regained for them.

Growing Pains

As the Bible college began to grow, Mathews soon realized that they would need a larger building and more land to house the students. The college didn't know how this would happen, since they had no money; but they put their faith in God and entrusted everything to His hands.

There was a Hindu real estate businessman who purchased a large tract of land, adjacent to a lake outside Udaipur. He divided the land into small plots and wanted to sell them as individual lots. At that time this area was remote because no good roads leading to it from the city had yet been made.

The businessman spent a lot of money, but because no one was showing any interest he was very upset. One day he came to Mathews and said, "Why don't you buy a piece of land? If a godly man like you purchases the first plot, then the whole parcel will sell."

Mathews said, "We can't afford a plot."

The man spread out his big tract map and said, "Okay, choose something and put some money on it. In this way you will get things going."

Mathews studied the map a few minutes. He noticed that while some of the plots stretched down to the lake, one plot did not front on the water. Mathews wrote on that parcel the word *Church*. He only had five hundred rupees, but he laid them all on the map. Then they parted.

A couple of weeks later the landowner called Mathews. He said, excitedly, "I sold all the plots, and they went for a big price once they saw the word *Church* on the map! Everyone thought that if a church is coming into that area, soon a school will be coming, and then the whole area will be developed. The plot you marked is yours. You can take your own time and give me the money in small installments as you get donations." He even reduced the cost, since he had made such a large profit.

But after the lots had all been sold, the government banned construction on the lakefront plots because that land was being preserved as a greenbelt to protect the lake. Since Mathews had taken a less desirable plot, the government ignored it. The developer had at first insisted that he take a lakeside plot, and he was almost tempted to do it. Thankfully God stopped him. If he had selected the seemingly more desirable plot, it would have been useless for a Bible college!

Two and one-half years later the final installment was made. Mathews paid two hundred thousand rupees for almost two acres, which was very cheap. The worth of the property today is far greater than that.

"According to your faith let it be to you" (Matthew 9:29). God blessed Mathews' faith, and once again He did the impossible. He knew that His Name would be glorified through what the future would bring on that miraculous plot of land!

Bible College Construction

The church now had land on which to build a Bible college, but they still had no money to build one. However, God was at work. Later that same year, Thampy Mathews paid a visit. He had visited the Bible school a few times before, just to see how the students lived and to get a feel for the Bible school that he had helped to start.

When Thampy saw that the old Manohar Bhawan was still being used to house the Bible school, he told Mathews, "Your family needs some privacy. The children are growing up, and these Bible school boys are staying here with you. You should pray for a new Bible school building."

Mathews lamented, "I can't bother to think about a new building, because I have enough struggle every day just *running* the school."

As Thampy was leaving to return to his home, he handed Mathews eighteen thousand rupees (around $600), which he had collected from his friends across the gulf. Putting the money in Mathews' hands, he said, "Pastor Mathews, we have the land, wonderfully provided by God. Now the Lord has given this money for a building. Keep it, and the Lord will help us to begin construction."

Mathews laughed at that statement in the same way Sarah did when she heard the promise from God of a son, because it would take far more than 18,000 rupees to build a college. Then he checked himself and said, "Praise the Lord. May the Lord bless you. I will put this money in the bank."

A few months later another piece of the puzzle fell into place in a very strange yet marvelous way. A young man named James appeared at Mathews' home one day. After introducing himself he said, "I am a civil engineer from Banswara (about one hundred miles south of Udaipur), where I had a job in a cement factory. The Lord told me one day, 'You must leave your job and construct buildings for My ministry!'" Mathews' attention was fully captured at this point.

"God also told me this," James continued: "'You are to build a four-storey building for a servant of Mine in Rajasthan.' So I prayed about it, and then I mentioned it to my pastor. He told me, 'There is a pastor in Udaipur who is praying for a Bible school building. Maybe that is where the Lord is directing you.' So that is why I came to see you."

Then this young Christian bachelor said another very strange thing. "Pastor Mathews, I resigned my job, and I have come here to start constructing that four-story building for you."

Mathews laughed in the same way he did when Thampy Mathews told him to save for a new college. He said, "Brother, you are wonderful! It's good that the Lord told you to build church buildings for Him, but you shouldn't have resigned your job. By staying at that job you could have helped to build many church buildings."

But the man stated resolutely, "The Lord *told* me to resign the job."

James had no money himself, and the eighteen thousand rupees that Mathews had in the bank were not enough to even start a building. But Mathews invited the zealous engineer into his home as a guest anyway because he could tell that James was full of faith and had a burning passion for God.

A couple of days later James asked Mathews, "Pastor, how much money do you have?"

"Around eighteen thousand rupees," was Mathews' reply.

What James said next surprised Mathews. "I know many steel and cement dealers in Udaipur because I used to purchase construction materials from them for our cement factory. These dealers know me. If you give me the eighteen thousand rupees, I will use the money for making down payments to dealers. Then we can get the steel and cement we need, and we can begin construction."

Mathews was silent for a few moments. He thought to himself, *That's a very good idea. This fellow is full of faith, and I shouldn't disappoint him.* So he said, "Okay, Brother James, let's do that."

James got to work right away and contacted some supply dealers in town. Since he was known and respected, they agreed to his proposal. They said, "If you want to build a church, take whatever you want. Then whatever money you receive as you go, you can give to us, and we will keep on delivering materials."

The congregation in Udaipur had outgrown Manohar Bhawan; so on Sunday mornings they rented the city hall for worship. One day a thought came to Mathews. He told James, "When you build the Bible school it should have a large chapel where we can have our Sunday meetings. And also add a couple of rooms for my family, because we don't want to have to rent another house when we move there."

James said, "Pastor, the Lord told me to lay the foundation for *four floors!*"

Mathews replied, "Just build one floor. Even one floor will cost several hundred thousand rupees."

James thought for a moment, and then said, "Well, then when you lay the foundation it should be strong enough to support four levels."

Mathews couldn't imagine that they would ever be able to build four floors; but that's what the Lord told James to do, and Mathews wasn't going to argue with the Lord! So James' idea was agreed upon.

One fine morning all the church members gathered together to begin the foundation for the building complex. With much struggle and many days of fasting and prayer, they diligently worked on the building, eighty-five feet long and forty feet wide. A few times they ran out of money, and the dealers troubled them because the money was overdue. But miraculously, often at the last moment, a gift would come from some friends. In this way, laboring day after day, they completed the building, with a chapel and the apartment for Mathews' family. In 1985, two years after construction began, Mathews, Mary, and their children said good-bye to Manohar Bhawan and moved into their new home.

But now their faith was to be tested severely. Shortly after the first floor was completed, city officials came and informed Mathews that the building was built illegally, without proper permission. They imposed a stay order stating that construction must stop and the rest of the land must be left for agriculture. The city government had decided to demolish the building, and they were not allowed to place even one more brick on it. They received the notice fifteen days prior to the planned demolition.

Then some other officials came and posted a notice announcing the date of demolition, and they told them that the police would check periodically to make sure construction was not being secretly carried out. The city claimed that Mathews hadn't applied for formal permission. But in fact the land was not within the city limits when they began construction, so there was no need to go to city authorities. However, the city expanded its borders, and this development was absorbed into the city limit.

The authorities had already demonstrated that they had the power to demolish the building. Near the lake there had been a beautiful new building that had just been finished; but the owner of that building had also built it without proper permission. Workers came with bulldozers and completely razed it. Mathews had seen what happened, and he knew that their building was next. The believers were broken and dismayed.

It appeared those years of prayer and hard physical labor, not to mention a great deal of money, were all going to waste. So the church decided to fast and pray in faith, and appeal to the court of Heaven for mercy—confident that God would take up their case.

Soon, the fifteen days to demolition had dwindled to five. That night some of the church leaders were praying with Mathews in his living room, and as they prayed, the Lord once again gave Mathews a *rhema,* this time from Psalms 55:22: "Cast your burden on the Lord and He shall sustain you; He shall never permit the righteous to be moved."

That message of hope entered Mathews' heart very powerfully, especially the words *never be moved*. They gave him great courage and confidence in the Lord. He announced to the five or six men who were praying with him, "Brothers, let us not worry. The Lord says that He will not allow His righteous ones to be moved. The Lord will not move this building."

The Bible school students were worshipping in the chapel at this time. Mathews walked to the chapel and told them, "Let us all pray. The Lord will do something for us."

Then there were only four more days left. After receiving the promise from the Lord, Mathews believed it and thanked God for it, but he didn't know just what to do. Then he remembered that there was a Muslim official in the city office. This man was the officer who would give the order to reduce the new Bible school to rubble.

Now in India, Muslims have special sympathy for Christians. Because both of them are minorities, they often help each other. With this thought in mind, Mathews developed a plan. He found out where the official's residence was and went there that very night. When the man came to the door, Mathews introduced himself and said, "Sir, you have to help us."

The man asked, "Why did you come to my home? I cannot help your building now. It's a hopeless case. You did an illegal thing."

Mathews replied, "You know that we didn't need a permit when we began; and if we had applied to your office we wouldn't have received permission. Then we could never build anything."

He thought a moment and said, "Yes, that's right."

"That is why we built it. We were trusting in God that He would do something about it."

Then the man began to laugh. "How will God help you when you did a wrong thing?"

Mathews knew that he was a deeply religious man, so he said, "Sir, the land was purchased and the building was constructed with the help of many godly people. We are praying right now for the building to stand (being a Muslim, the official also believed in the power of prayer). You are also a man who believes in a god, and you also believe in Isa (Jesus). Isa is your prophet, so you should help save this building because it was built for Him."

Mathews saw that the official's face had taken on a very serious look, and that he was deep in thought. A few moments later he said, "Okay, if there is anything I can do to help you, I will do it. But I don't know what I can do. If I remain alive for the next four days I will try my best."

Mathews quickly replied, "I'll pray to Isa, the prophet, to keep you alive for the next few days so that you can help this cause."

They both laughed together at this, and then the official served tea. After a short time Mathews bid the man good night and left.

The next morning the Muslim official came to see the building, and he and Mathews went up to the flat roof. He was visibly upset because this beautiful building was about to be demolished by his own words. There was not another building like it in the whole area. He knew it was to be used for prayer to Isa Nabi (Jesus, the prophet), so he wanted no part in its demolition.

As he paced back and forth on the roof, he spotted a date written in the cement. He asked, "What is that date for?"

Mathews had forgotten that he had written the date there. He said, "That is the date when this roof was poured. I wrote it there in the wet cement with my own finger."

The Muslim man queried, "Are you sure?"

"Yes, yes! You can read it."

From a file folder the official was carrying, he pulled out a copy of the demolition order, just like the one that was pasted on the wall. He studied the order, examining every word again and again. Finally he exclaimed, "This is wonderful! Your prayer to Isa Nabi is answered! The stay order for the building should have been made before the roof was completed." According to the city code, if construction was to be halted, a stay order had to be posted at least ten days before the roof was finished.

The Muslim continued, "Unfortunately for our department, the stay order was set for a date later than the day you finished the roof."

Once again the Christian and the Muslim laughed together. Mathews praised God and the Muslim praised Allah, and they both were very happy. The official drove to his office and reported to his superior: "Sir, the date on our stay order is after the roof casting was done. What can we do? Our hands are tied." Everyone in the office was stunned.

Later Mathews put up a cross on the building and wrote underneath it, *Christian Prayer Temple,* to show that the building was used for that purpose.

When the day that the building was supposed to be demolished finally dawned, the believers still were a little uncertain about what might happen. They feared that the city officials might contrive a reason to tear down the building anyway. With the cross and sign in place, the Bible school students and teachers all gathered for prayer and singing, so that everyone would know it was a church. The police did come, but they left soon after.

The fact that the Christians' building was not demolished fueled much talk in the town, which in turn created favorable publicity for the college. The local newspaper people, who were very opposed to Christianity, were ashamed; the Lord had performed a great miracle.

Chapter Sixteen

Highways and Byways

Growing up in the Mathews' home did present a few problems for the children. Their home was always open to visitors, and visitors came frequently. At times the children had to use the kitchen table in their small apartment at the Bible college in Udaipur to study on, because someone else was occupying their rooms. At other times they went to a friend's house to study, because even the kitchen table might not be available.

However, with such a steady flow of new faces, Grace, Glory, and Paul were exposed to wonderful lessons that taught them how to love all kinds of people. In addition, they experienced the zeal of many of God's servants who were intent on bringing the Gospel to the lost of the North and to plant churches wherever they could.

Church planting was often a family affair for Thomas, Mary, and their three children. Mathews knew that actions usually speak louder than words, so he and Mary made their mission experience one big open schoolroom for Grace, Glory, and Paul. In this way the children could witness God's love for the whole world and develop for themselves hearts of compassion for these desperately needy people. Their lives revolved around ministering to people, both at home near Udaipur and in distant villages on the field.

One summer during the school vacation, Mathews and Mary took the children along with them to the interior villages of Maharashtra and Gujarat. Early in the morning, they packed food and clothing into suitcases. Having no vehicle of their own, they boarded a crowded bus, along with other members of the ministry team. They were headed to a village many miles off the highway in the Western Ghat Mountains of Gujarat. Since the buses only traveled the main roads, they got off at a prearranged point that was closest to the village.

There they met a brother from the village who would serve as their guide. Then they walked... and walked... balancing luggage on their heads. After awhile one of the children asked their father, "How far is it to the village?" Mathews told them to ask their guide.

So they said, "Uncle,[11] how far is it to the village?"

He pointed to a distant mountain and said, "See that mountain over there? At the tip of the mountain is where the village lies."

The group kept on walking, but the mountain never seemed to get any closer. Then they all sat down under a tree and had a snack. Sometimes if a mango tree was nearby, they might squeeze the juice out of the fruit and drink it to keep from getting sunstroke.

When the base of the mountain was finally reached, there were still no houses or people. Up the mountain they climbed, and the children said, "Where is it now?"

Their guide answered, "Its just beyond that tree up ahead."

On they pressed, and finally, after starting their hike at ten in the morning, they saw the village ahead. It was 6:00 p.m.

The children were murmuring about the long walk to this dry, dusty village, and one of them questioned her parents: "Why do you take so much trouble coming all the way up here to these people?"

Their father replied, "There is no one else to tell them about Jesus. Someone has to come and tell them. That is what God requires of His people. God has given us this privilege of coming to this area and getting to know these people. We're just obeying the Lord."

When they finally arrived in the center of the village, Mathews and Mary encouraged their children to participate in reaching these people by singing children's songs in Hindi. When they began to sing, the village children ran to listen. Many of these songs were related to a Bible passage, and they would do actions that would help to tell the story. After distributing candy, they told the children to bring their parents back in the evening to hear more singing and listen to a talk. So in the early evening the children, bringing their parents, gathered around a tree in the center of the village and listened to the Gospel and to spiritual songs. The Holy Spirit moved among the people, and many gave their hearts to Jesus.

The Mathews children saw for themselves that Jesus died for everyone. John 3:16 became a reality as they watched the love of Jesus changing lives. The blessings they reaped far outweighed the disadvantages. Through these experiences and many more, Grace, Glory, and Paul watched their own parents cast all their cares on the Lord for every detail of life. With such lessons as these lived out before their eyes, God was equipping them for their future roles in the Native Missionary Movement organization.

As mentioned earlier, Mary and a team of other women had opened many of these villages to the Gospel. Going from village to village, they taught the women how to dress modestly, since many women in this area wore very little clothing. Basic hygiene was also taught. They brought soap and clothes and showed them how to wash their hair and trim their nails and how to keep the children clean and dressed appropriately for the weather. Along the way, the Gospel would be shared with them. The village women appreciated learning these things, and they became more open to hearing the message of Jesus after seeing the love of Jesus in action.

Sometimes when meetings were held, the village sorcerer would come. At first it might be out of curiosity, but as more and more people accepted Christ his very livelihood was jeopardized. Then he would become angry and threaten the people with severe consequences.

All Things to All People

Mathews always tried to respect the individual cultural practices of a village. For example, in some villages of the North they had no banks in which to keep their money safe. Often the women in such villages would take whatever small amount of cash they might receive and buy silver jewelry to wear. Then they could sell the jewelry whenever ready cash was needed.

In ordinary situations when women came to Christ, they would be instructed that wearing ornate jewelry was not in keeping with a meek and quiet spirit. However, in these cultural settings where jewelry often represented their life savings, nothing was said to these new converts.

Many times women would attend meetings wearing bracelets made of black thread, or even metal chains. In the Hindu religion the priest was involved in black magic. This black-magic priesthood was an inherited position, passed on from one generation to the next in the same family. Much power and wealth was associated with these village priests. Villagers would come to them for help, usually for some sort of healing for themselves or another family member, or even their cattle, which represented their only source of income.

The black magician would perform a ritual and then tie a string or chain around the person's wrist, or sometimes even their waist. This chain served as a symbol that their problem had been removed and that they would have no further trouble. In return, they would give the priest money, or perhaps a chicken.

Many times women who wore such bracelets would be invited to a church service. When a call was given to accept Jesus as Saviour and Lord, some of them might respond. After the meeting many of these black-string bracelets would be found lying on the floor, because immediately upon being converted, women would often be convicted that the practice behind these bracelets was evil. They discovered right away that Jesus truly does set the captives free.

Chapter Seventeen

Labor On: A Time of Growth

Go, labor on; spend and be spent,
Thy joy to do the Father's will;
It is the way the Master went;
Should not the servant tread it still?
— Horatius Bonar

The spiritual fields of northern India had been fallow for centuries, choked in the bondage of sin and evil spirits, when Thomas Mathews answered the call to make its people his people. To get an idea of what Mathews faced at this point, imagine that you have a home garden plot with excellent soil, twenty feet by forty feet—a good size garden for a family. You plant seeds, water, fertilize, weed...and wait. Then you reap the reward of your efforts.

Now it so happens that next to your property lies a one thousand acre field blessed with the same nutritious soil as your own small garden. This field has never been cultivated; no seeds have ever been planted here; no careful weeding and fertilizing. Yet in that soil lies the same potential as that which blessed you with such a fine yield. What a tremendous harvest could come from a garden that size!

All of northern India a vast, productive garden for God—
that was Mathews' vision. The Spirit of God had touched the
hearts of a few hungry souls in the "family garden" of Rajasthan.
However, the prophecy that he would bring the Gospel to
thousands of souls representing many languages in the vast
acreage of the rest of the North burned more intensely in his
heart following the entrance into Gujarat and Maharashtra; for
now at last he saw the bright light of Jesus beginning to spread.

Mathews needed to learn much, starting out as a newly
committed nineteen-year-old. But over the years Jesus was
patiently and gently molding him into His own likeness so that
he could see the situation in northern India through His
compassionate eyes. He had witnessed the compassion of Jesus
in his own home while growing up. Now he was learning it
himself.

Rajasthan had been a wonderful training ground for him.
Learning to relate to villagers opened the door for his compassion
to flow out. However, he soon realized the enormity of the
mission field of northern India, and that in order to reach all
those unreached people, different methods needed to be
employed than those used in the past. It was clear that a handful
of cross-cultural evangelists using traditional methods were no
match for the great number of lost souls in the North. Many had
tried; many had failed.

Other missionaries had answered God's call to "Go," but
Mathews had seen the tragedy of not discipling new believers
after conversion. It was painful seeing these young Christians
try to stand alone against the satanic attacks that soon came.
These newly converted villagers knew next to nothing about
God and His plan for them, other than their need for salvation
and Who it was that did the saving. Now they needed to be
nurtured in the ways of their Lord.

Peter admonished "those who have obtained like precious
faith" to "grow in the grace and knowledge of [their] Lord and

Savior Jesus Christ" (2 Peter 1:12; 3:18). But Mathews and his friends couldn't personally mentor everyone who was coming to Christ. In order to nurture brothers and sisters in the deeper things of their Lord Jesus, a church was needed where these babes in Christ could be given love, spiritual food, fellowship, and encouragement. This was the "teach" or "disciple" part of Christ's Great Commission. The end of this discipling, hopefully, would produce maturing believers who were dead to sin and alive through the power of Christ, willing to give themselves to others, as He did for them.

Being a cross-cultural missionary himself, Mathews knew that the indigenous people themselves were far more effective in reaching their own regions and cultures than cross-cultural evangelists alone. If these people who were being converted were discipled to share the love of Jesus in their own villages, what might be the result? Instead of a few evangelists, there could be hundreds...or even thousands!

From Theory to Practice

After the success of Maharashtra and Gujarat, the momentum began to pick up. The new Christians there became disciples. Churches were established, and they were taught about God's plan for a perfect world of love between Himself and the ones His Son had created. They learned that God's glorious vision was marred by sin, and that Jesus had come to show the world the right way to live. He went so far as to shed His blood and die to buy back those he loved. Even more astounding was the fact that Jesus would live inside them to be their life; they would be a new creation.

But they were also taught that Jesus wanted to take full control of their lives in order to fulfill His Father's plan for them, for the Father wanted to use them, just like He used Jesus Himself. Jesus loved His disciples; they would love other believers. Jesus loved His enemies; they would love theirs too.

Jesus did everything to please His Father; they would also. Jesus commanded that they follow in His steps; they would obey and follow.

Mathews recognized that these native people knew the language and were familiar with the culture, which gave them a greater identification with their people. Since they understood the local problems and differences, they were able to identify with what their neighbors were going through. They could communicate the Gospel far more effectively than could the ones who had reached out to them from Rajasthan.

Soon the villagers were taught and encouraged to the point that they began to share with others what Jesus had done for them. Before long, neighboring villages were hearing the glad news of Jesus; not only from Mathews or his team, but also from those they had won for the Lord.

In time, the number of churches and believers began to mushroom, just like the growth of the Church in the first century. Church planting continued in Rajasthan, Gujarat, and Maharashtra, and spread to the surrounding states, including Madhya Pradesh and Orissa. Churches planted; believers nurtured in the love of Christ witnessing to their own villagers and to those in neighboring towns and villages who, in turn, would repeat the steps: The native missionary concept was growing into a native missionary *movement*.

Bible College and Missionary Training Centers

In 1993 the Bible college was suffering through a time of deep need. For several weeks the students ate poor quality food. Mathews had a heavy debt to pay to the grocery store, so he didn't dare go there to shop. The faculty and the students spent more time asking God to provide for their needs, but there was no improvement in the situation. In fact, the day came when the only thing left to eat or drink for the teachers, students, and Mathews' family was black tea.

Mathews and Mary were so discouraged after seeing the condition of some of the students that they closed the door to their room and cried out to the Lord with tears. They asked God to show them His will at that difficult hour, whether to keep the Bible college open or not. If He didn't, they would close it down for good.

The next morning the Bible college girls went out to a field and picked a lot of leaves. Then they made a soup out of them, putting the leaves in boiling water and adding some spices and onions. It was then served to the students and faculty. Though the students knew the financial crisis of the college very well, they did not murmur or grumble. Instead, with one accord they prayed to the God who can provide in mysterious ways.

Mathews and Mary had shared their experiences of faith and God's provisions with the students in classes, in meetings, and even person-to-person. Now the students were having a first-hand experience in suffering and in living by faith.

The next morning the postman arrived at the usual hour. But this time as he entered the college gate, all eyes were focused on him.[12] He brought with him an envelope from Dubai (across the Arabian Gulf) addressed to Thomas Mathews.

With eager anticipation Mathews took the letter and opened it. Inside was a bank draft for 10,855 rupees with this mysterious note: "Dear Pastor Mathews, Greetings! This is all I have. Hope it will be a help to your ministry. Your brother in Christ."

It was a heaven-sent gift indeed! The sender had deliberately remained anonymous, so Mathews wrote to the bank for his address; but there was no response. He was very disappointed because he could not send that precious brother a word of gratitude and share with him the desperate need that his wonderful gift had met.

Two years later, Mathews visited Dubai and preached at meetings organized by many churches that met together to hear him. He told the story of the miraculous gift and the anonymous donor. Hoping that he would be in the audience, he encouraged whoever it was to meet him privately after the meeting. But he was disappointed again and left still wondering. Whoever gave the money may not be revealed until the day of the Lord's return. But on that day this dear brother will receive his reward openly from the Lord because he did not desire the praise or thanks of men (Matthew 6:2–4).

Navapur Convention

"Gather all the congregation together" (Leviticus 8:3).

These new believers lived in a world that was hostile toward them, and the leaders sensed a need for them to fellowship together to encourage one another in love. In October 1981, around one hundred people in the greater region gathered together in Navapur, Maharashtra. During the next few days they worshipped together, listened to teaching from the Word, sang praises, prayed, and encouraged each other. At night they used a kerosene lantern to give light. The sessions were long, but no one minded, for all were there for the common purpose of worshipping and glorifying Jesus.

These meetings were so meaningful that it was decided to make the gathering an annual event. In the following years, more and more saints traveled the dusty roads by foot, ox cart, or motorized vehicle to Navapur. In time some people were traveling for days, covering hundreds of miles, just to share the joy of like-minded fellowship. We, with sometimes dozens or even hundreds of churches within a reasonable distance, find it difficult to understand how meaningful such a gathering could be to these northern Indian Christians.

The Birth of the Printing Ministry

During those days, when the "hammer & sickle" was flying high in Kerala, Mathews thought, "Why not the "cross and the crown"? The cross and the crown of Christ were being suppressed by the hammer and sickle—the symbols of communism that flew on the Soviet flag—all over the Red empire. Mathews had a great desire to bring out a small periodical in English with the title, "Cross & Crown," but he had no money. When he shared his dream with a non-Christian printer-friend named Onkarlalji, he encouraged Mathews to do it. He said, "Go ahead and print whatever you want to print; you can pay me whenever you get the money. I'll also purchase paper for you."

At that time Mathews also met a man named P.C. Mathews (no relation), a chain smoker and an alcohol addict—almost a "hopeless case." He was attending an evening class with Mathews at the local college, and Mathews invited him to a Saturday Bible study. P.C. came to the small gathering, and as Mathews preached on Lazarus and the rich man, the Lord spoke to him. The following day in the Sunday service, P.C. Mathews stood up with tears in his eyes and invited Jesus into his heart. It was the turning point not only in his life and in his orthodox family, but also in the printing ministry.

Brother P.C. had a good job at the University of Udaipur in editing and publishing. Without consulting anybody, he resigned his job. His only aim was to help Mathews in some kind of publishing and printing work. Neither of the two had any money to start anything, nor did anyone else promise to help. However, a businessman from Bombay named J.D. Kamble came to Udaipur on business. Jesus had wonderfully transformed his life through Mathews' guidance, and Kamble was led to help them financially.

In 1977 the Lord led P.C. Mathews to a used, out-of-date, manual printing machine, which Kamble purchased. Besides bringing out the small Cross & Crown, they printed thousands of tracts in Hindi, the official national language of India.

In the early years, Mathews and his wife and children labored into the wee hours of the night, writing addresses and affixing postage stamps on all the copies of the magazine and doing all the mailing. Later P.C. joined them, and a few church members also helped them in their spare time.

Then they began to pray for an automatic printing press. God answered their prayers in a wonderful way. Their evangelist friend, Isaac Mathai of Jaipur, gave the necessary amount to purchase an automatic machine. After its installation, the printing work began to catch momentum. As the printing work increased, they felt the need for an offset machine. Three years later God answered their prayers and gave them a single-color offset machine.

In later years several Christian books written in Hindi were printed on their press. Up to that time hardly any Christian literature printed in Hindi was available. Mathews wrote a book in Hindi on Bible prophecies, which was well accepted. Hindi Bible correspondence courses were also printed in the print shop. In addition, a quarter of a million Hindi tracts were produced.

As the years flew by, they began to pray that the press would work day and night to produce Gospel literature in Hindi and other regional languages as well. They dreamed of printing Hindi literature, not by the hundred thousands of copies, but by tons and truckloads!

Children's Home and Schools

Children held a special place in the heart of Jesus, as recorded in Matthew 19:14: "Let the little children come to Me, and do not forbid them; for of such is the kingdom of heaven." He also used their humility and lack of personal ambition, in spite of the negative influence that surrounded them, to teach an object lesson to His disciples: "Unless you are converted and become as little children, you will by no means enter the kingdom of heaven" (Matthew 18:3).

It is tragic that children suffer because of the sin of the world. Nowhere is this sad truth more apparent than in India. India is home to over one billion people. Six hundred million of them live in *deep* poverty. Literally millions of Indian children live in filth, poverty, and hunger. Many of these little ones are abandoned to make it on their own—some three million in India's cities alone.

Most children there are born into families who have lived on the edge of starvation long before these new souls enter the world. When the need for food increases as the children get older, there is nothing left to give them. Many are tearfully set free by the parents to fend for themselves. In addition, India now ranks among the highest two or three countries in the world in AIDS cases, and millions of HIV-positive children are orphaned or abandoned as a result.

Mathews and Mary realized the need of taking care of native children when they confronted the helpless condition of a family in one of the villages. The mother had died of some sickness. The father was an alcoholic and did not care for the three children, who lived a pathetic life.

One day their grandfather brought his three grandchildren to the Mathews and asked if they could take care of them, since he could not trust the children with his drunken son. Thomas and Mary felt compassion for the children, and so they told the man that they would be happy to give them a home. So the children lived with them and went to school. Soon they chose to follow Jesus, and as the years went by, they found a trade so they could support themselves.

The first children's home was started in 1980 in Kotdad, Rajasthan, an area that was very primitive and without one Christian. When Mathews heard of that region, he wanted to bring them the Gospel, so he went there with Gospel tracts. The people of Kotdad told him he was not welcome to their village unless he could help them in making their children literate. So he prayed and came back, this time with a few more team members, and they started a literacy program.

Most of the villages didn't have schools, and if the parents went to do labor work during the day, the children were left to wander about with no purpose. Even though a few towns had a school, it was expensive for a family in the village to send a child there. If the mother or the father died, the children had to work in order to feed the family, and then they never had an opportunity to go to school.

Over time the literacy program developed into a children's home with a government-recognized school. Along with a basic education, the students were taught about the love of God, and many of them committed their lives to Jesus. As a result of this ministry, a young man named Veeram, one of the original children in that home, became the coordinator of the children's home in Kotdad. Before long, other homes were started.

Mobile Team/Film Ministry

Northern India spreads out across a vast landscape within its irregular borders. One can travel in the North more than 1,700 miles east to west and more than 1,200 miles north to south. Highways link the larger cities and towns, but the great majority of villages know nothing of paved roads to connect them. Many of these villages also lie in the midst of rough terrain.

As the ministry field of NMM expanded, it became apparent that the new churches needed more teaching and encouragement. Isolated because of long distances and slow transportation, the new Christians lacked fellowship with other believers, much like the early Church. The annual convention was a blessing, but it occurred only once a year.

However, if faster and more reliable transportation was available, these needs could be met more easily. The local churches could be helped as they reached out to neighboring villages. What if a team would travel by a Jeep-type vehicle, loaded with tracts and loudspeakers? This would reduce travel time and would pave the way for native missionaries to do their work.

The first of these teams, accompanied by Mathews, started out from Udaipur and went to the surrounding towns and villages where they had contacts. There they preached on dusty street corners, and they also carried the message of hope and peace from one house to the next.

The mobile teams also carried with them another tool, one that proved to be a mighty weapon in the war against bondage to sin. In those days the literacy rate of the entire country hovered around fifty percent, with the rural areas lagging far behind that dismal number. In order to more effectively communicate the Gospel to village people, the mobile teams began showing a film on the life of Christ that was based on the Book of Luke. Not surprisingly, the film met with great success, especially among the illiterate villagers of the North. Since movies are a popular medium in India, the locals responded eagerly when they were invited to a screening.

At first the Hindi translation of Campus Crusade for Christ's "Jesus film" was shown. That film was later translated and dubbed into two local dialects, Vagdi and Mewari, with the help of NMM workers. Later on the ministry began to show the film, "Man of Mercy," which also depicts the life of Jesus, but with Indian actors.

Soon this concept had spread to several surrounding states. In this way villages were opened to the Gospel, which allowed a pastor from a nearby village with an existing church to nurture the newly saved and continue the outreach. In time, a church would be established there as well, and the process instituted so long ago would repeat itself to the glory of God.

Medical Van Teams

In light of India's profound poverty and lack of nutrition, it's no surprise that health was a major concern in northern India. Mathews felt strongly that preaching the Gospel, not humanitarian aid, was God's highest priority for the most unreached of India. He knew that the lost souls needed Jesus, the True Bread from heaven and the healing Balm of Gilead, more than anything else. Yet his heart, fueled by the compassion of Jesus, ached when he saw the desperate circumstances of the northerners, whom he loved. His family, too, often felt the pangs of true hunger—pangs that few in the developed world could identify with.

In the late 1980's NMM instituted a new ministry aimed at meeting the spiritual needs of the villagers while focusing on health issues. Medical and dental professionals from all over India, and other countries as well, were encouraged to donate their time to be a part of a mobile health clinic.

When enough help was available, medical teams were assembled. These teams entered a village and set up a temporary clinic. Then, while examining and treating dental problems and various illnesses and ailments, team members shared the love of Jesus with their patients. Later on, they made house visits as well. The native people were impressed by the willingness of these Christians to comfort them in their time of need. In this way many hearts were touched after seeing such a demonstration of love.

Persecution Increases

Remember the word that I said to you, 'A servant is not greater than his master.' If they persecuted Me, they will also persecute you   (John 15:20).

Mathews knew that he was preaching a radical message in a hostile land. But he rejoiced in the persecution that was sure to come, instead of getting discouraged. It simply meant that he was following his Master's example and command. To Mathews, a godly life was one in which Jesus was given control to continue His work; and if He was persecuted for it, then Mathews considered it an honor to be like his Lord.

The privilege of being persecuted was engrained in the hearts and minds of the new Christians of northern India, and they were usually tested immediately. Rejection by one's family and friends was sure to come, and that created tremendous hardship; for along with it came a severing of all religious and cultural ties. In other words, everything that was familiar vanished. Employment disappeared. Sometimes privileges such as health care and education disappeared as well.

The commitment a person made to follow Christ came with a high cost. Much soul searching went into such a decision. But counting the cost made these new believers intensely zealous to work for Christ. They had found Someone who loved them— One who took away their load of sin and gave them peace as an exchange. He broke their chains of idol worship, and they in turn desired and were determined to introduce this Jesus to mothers, fathers, siblings, friends—everyone!

Bihar state in northeast India is situated below the country of Nepal. The Ganges River runs through a large, fertile, agricultural plain, but the tribal people live in the less-fertile southern region. Most of the southerners are animists— believers in ancestral worship and the offering of sacrifices to certain rocks, trees, and other objects.

In the tribal village of Dubalia, a man named Sathish and his family heard the Gospel of Jesus and decided to follow Him. But animists believed that Sathish and his family polluted the atmosphere of the village.

Regrettably, when this happened Sathish was forced to sign an agreement that forfeited his family's land. His wife, Shiva Devi, was tonsured (shaved), and lime powder was applied to her face; then she was paraded around for all to see. Finally the couple and their three sons were forced from their home, driven from their village, and barred from ever returning. Sadly, Sathish's father and mother were among those who drove them from Dubalia.

Such heartrending accounts became commonplace as the Gospel advanced across the northern frontier. But its bearers went rejoicing, for they knew theirs was the Kingdom of heaven.

As time went by and the eighties turned the corner into the nineties, the movement continued to expand. The Gospel probed new frontiers, and soon churches were being planted in Orissa, Bihar, Madhya Pradesh, and fourteen other states in North India. Mathews rejoiced to see what the Lord was doing, but he was never content. The knowledge that there were millions of souls crowding the villages and towns who had never heard about Jesus prevented contentment from creeping in.

Chapter Eighteen

Spend and Be Spent: A Time of Grief

When the new millennium dawned, Mathews had been laboring and "spending" in the North for more than thirty-six years. These were years spent loving the people of the North as his own; years seeing the birth of a strong movement of the Holy Spirit among these people; years filled with hunger, persecution, long days, sleepless nights—yet years of happiness. These years had also taken a toll on his body.

After moving to the North, Mathews developed asthma, and the subsequent years of fighting this ailment weakened his heart, along with the responsibility of leadership, a torturous schedule, and years without adequate nourishment. Now in his late fifties, he suffered two mild heart attacks, one while visiting the United States. He had labored on, and now he was almost spent.

God had poured out His Spirit on the North, but in so doing, the scope of the ministry had grown as well. This meant more planning, more visiting, more teaching, more preaching—tasks that Mathews relished but could no longer accomplish on his own as the leader of the organization called Native Missionary Movement.

Mathews knew that his time on earth was drawing to a close, and that the structure of leadership was woefully inadequate to meet the demands that the future was sure to bring. Several brothers had been helping to administer the work, but Mathews felt that more were needed.

However, the "perks" of being in leadership with NMM were questionable when compared with most Christian organizations. There was no salary—not one of the leaders received any pay. They relied on living by faith, trusting that Jesus would meet their needs, in the same way that the brothers and sisters they ministered to lived. In fact, the entire organization spent not one cent on salaries for administration. Every penny went to the field to give a meager support to the missionaries, who seldom could find employment in the poverty-stricken villages where they labored.

But by faith God raised up men to lead who had learned first to serve. They understood that the Lord's call to deny self and follow Him was meant for everyone, including themselves, and not only for the front line missionaries. Many of them had started out as missionaries and also shared with Mathews the importance of planting churches to disciple new believers.

Going Home

The annual convention held a special place in Mathews' heart. Each year he would welcome the ever-increasing crowd of believers gathered from an ever-increasing number of states and foreign countries.

The November 2005 convention in Navapur, Maharashtra was a special one, for this was its twenty-fifth anniversary. The convention had come to a glorious conclusion, and those who organized and implemented it were exhausted from the staggering amount of preparation that goes into hosting fifty thousand people for six days.

Yet even as the closing prayer was, as it were, ringing in the ears of the worshippers, Mathews was, as always, thinking ahead.

He had been planning yet another outreach to yet another unreached area, and he shared with the leadership the deep need for more missionaries in the North. Then it was on to Udaipur in Rajasthan, where it all started. Mathews preached there on Sunday, November 20th, and for revival meetings the next few days as well.

That Sunday he preached a prophetic message titled "Rehoboth," meaning *room, expansion*, from the Book of Genesis. In it he encouraged the believers by saying that the Lord was going to expand the ministry in the coming years in incredible ways—even beyond the borders of India. He wasn't able to share all that he had prepared, so he closed by saying, "If God keeps me alive, I'll deliver the second phase of this sermon next time." However, the God who pulled him out of the water so long ago had different plans. That "next time" was not to come.

Wednesday, the twenty-third of November, dawned. Mathews prayed with another pastor, then he packed and said goodbye to Mary, his lifelong partner, one more time. Leaving for Delhi, he planned to spend the night there and join some others for the train ride to Amritsar in Punjab, where he was to speak at a leader's conference and address a Gospel rally.

That evening in Delhi he ate dinner and spent time in conversation with his hosts, asking them to wake him early so he could catch the 7:30 a.m. train. Then he went to bed.

But sometime in the night, Thomas Mathews heard his beloved Master, Jesus Christ, say, "Behold, I come! (Revelation 22:12 KJV). Well done thou good and faithful servant" (Matthew 25:21). And instead of catching a train, he was caught up to heaven.

In April 1963, a nineteen-year-old boy responded to God's call for North India and traveled from his home in Kerala to Delhi. From there it was on to Rajasthan to spread the Gospel of the glory of God in the face of Jesus among the people he loved. When he died, he still had that first train ticket tucked inside his Malayalam Bible.

In November 2005, sixty-one-year-old Thomas Mathews traveled this time from Rajasthan to Delhi. And it was from Delhi again that he left; not back to Kerala, but this time to heaven, to rest from his labor and spend eternity in the presence of Jesus. What a wonderful home going!

Sympathy poured into the family's home in Udaipur when the news of Mathews' death became known. Mary and the children received messages of tribute and compassion from around the world, and thousands of people from all over India came to the NMM headquarters in Udaipur to say one last "Good-bye."

Over the years Mathews had traveled extensively overseas, preaching the Gospel and sharing what God was doing in India. Many pastors whom he had met had traveled to northern India and participated in the work, teaching in the Bible schools and traveling about preaching in the villages.

One such pastor from Canada wrote these words of encouragement and love to Mary: "Your wonderful husband and you have not only made a difference in India, but around the world. We love you very much and share in the loss of our beloved friend, and your dear husband. I count it a great privilege to have known and loved him. His influence will forever make a difference in my life. He has made me smile, he has inspired me, he has challenged me: and more than anything, he showed me what it looks like to be like Jesus in so many ways."

One of the most touching testimonials came from Kamal Masih. He wrote, "I am one of those persons who persecuted Pastor Thomas Mathews in Kevadia, Rajasthan, and dragged him to the police station. But by God's grace I received baptism with his own hands, and now I am one of his closest co-workers."

People from many denominations and all walks of life, from peasants to members of Parliament attended the funeral, for Jesus' love had poured out of Mathews into the varied lives of all he met. K. P. Yohannan, the head of Gospel for Asia, had spent time with Mathews and Mary in the North when he was only seventeen years old, while traveling with an Operation Mobilization team. Remembering his friend as he closed the funeral, he said, "I do not know very many Christian leaders who have lived forty-two years of consistent life and backed their teaching with their lives...A few hours before his travel to Delhi, I talked with him. All our conversations were always about the work of God."

It was fitting, perhaps even prophetic that K.P. should finish with words that so accurately yet simply summed up what drove the vision of this beloved man: "If in some way God would allow Thomas Mathews to come now and talk to us...he would say 'Love Him with all your heart; serve Him with all your might; please Him in all your ways, and live every single day in the light of eternity...' He would say, 'Don't look back. Don't slow down. Give all you have to Jesus for His glory.'"

A Legacy

Why did Thomas Mathews have such a profound impact on the people of North India? Simply put, he believed in Jesus, and he obeyed Him; he lived the life he taught. Each time he was hard pressed, he never became discouraged. Instead, he cried out to God, and God heard his cry. When God showed him how to win the North by evangelizing, planting churches, and discipling new believers, he obeyed at a tremendous cost to his safety and health. His faith increased each time he saw the Lord save, heal, and love these people trapped so long in the bondage of false religion and evil spirits, and every time he watched them apply the Word to their own lives.

As Mathews learned to know and love the Lord Jesus more intimately, he leaned more and more on the power of His indwelling Spirit, and less and less on his own abilities. God used him mightily because he humbled himself to be used. The vision—bringing the Gospel of Jesus to hundreds of millions of Indians—looked impossible. But Thomas had faith that God's love combined with God's power could overcome any obstacle.

Because Jesus commanded His disciples to follow Him no matter what it cost, Mathews took it literally. He knew that Jesus meant what He said when He said, "Whoever desires to come after Me, let him deny himself, and take up his cross, and follow Me. For whoever desires to save his life will lose it, but whoever loses his life for My sake and the Gospel's will save it" (Mark 8:34–35). Because he laid down his own agenda, his personal desires, and his ambitions, he received the joy that the world cannot give.

Simple faith and obedience unleashed the power of God in a dark land. When Mathews went home to be with the Lord, Native Missionary Movement had seen more than two hundred thousand people commit their lives to Jesus, more than one thousand churches planted, and more than one thousand pastors raised up, most of whom were saved through the NMM ministry. In addition there were all the previously mentioned ministries that had been put into place to meet the many needs.

Today Mathews shares eternity not only with his Lord, but also with those "mothers and fathers, sisters and brothers" that God gave to him while he sojourned on earth.

God showed Thomas Mathews an open door. All Mathews did was walk through it—God did the rest. Thomas Mathews showed us Jesus.

PART THREE:

NATIVE MISSIONARY
MOVEMENT
TODAY

Chapter Nineteen

India Today

*I*f you lived in India, you would be surrounded by a beautiful yet contrasting landscape. This elephant head-shaped country is framed by the soaring Himalayan Mountain Range to the north, and by oceans on the west, south, and east. Marked by both scorching deserts and steaming rain forests, it sees rain-swollen monsoon winds that flood the flat valleys, and tropical breezes that cool the coasts.

Where you would live and the lifestyle you lived would depend on your social standing, or caste; for the human imprint on India is characterized by contrasts as well. The elite of India's high-caste citizens live in luxurious metropolitan homes, mostly in or near the big cities, while all around them the outcasts grovel in squalor that is unparalleled in the world. Streets and alleys lined with shacks and lean-tos surround the large cities, which also serve as "home" to the world's largest concentration of homeless, wandering children.

If you lived in India, the natural wonder of the snow-capped mountains and the man-made beauty of the Taj Mahal would be dimmed by countless sacred cows moving aimlessly among half-starving villagers, or sacred rats nibbling at precious food supplies.

Indian universities produce the second largest number of science-related professionals in the world, as well as excellent doctors and surgeons. High-tech businesses are booming. Yet the vast sea of low caste and untouchable rural people—uneducated, illiterate, and unemployed—dwarfs their numbers. Hundreds of millions of destitute villagers either eke out enough from the land to stay alive, or flood the cities looking for work—and finding none.

English is the primary language of the wealthy because of its economic and political influence. In fact English is an official associate language of India. The poor, most of them in that 70 percent of the population living in rural areas, suffer under the bondage of one of the highest illiteracy rates in the world. Unable to read and write, and bound by their tribal languages, millions of people on the Indian subcontinent remain trapped in desperate poverty—prisoners to slave labor, debt bondage, and exploitation by those in higher levels of society.

Dalits—*the oppressed.* That's the name given to 300 million Indians who were the former "untouchables"—those considered to be so impure that they were *below* the lowest caste. For the Dalits and another 300 million low-caste people, very little has changed since the nation became a democracy over 50 years ago and declared equal human rights for all citizens. The reason is not an inadequate constitution, but a prevalent 3,000 year-old religious belief system that determines the value of an individual and what he can do in life based on the caste in which he was born. And from this caste there is no escape possible, regardless of what he may achieve in life.

One other area of contrast looms over the scene in India: the contrast within the Hindu religious system itself. Eighty-five percent of Indians are Hindus, worshipping any number of gods from among literally thousands. They worship at ornate temples, pay homage to intricate statues, and perform in colorful and elaborate rituals and festivals. But while Hindus are striving to obtain a better position in their reincarnated lives, they practice "purification" rites in polluted rivers in the world; and they follow teachings that bring them into the bondage of caste and its evils: poverty, hunger, illiteracy, and despair.

In many ways northern India today is in the same desperate bondage as it was when Thomas Mathews first stepped off the train in Udaipur, Rajasthan, in 1963—with one dramatic exception. The Gospel of Jesus Christ is spreading across the land and bringing souls out of bondage at a mushrooming rate. The Lord Jesus is no respecter of persons; He loves all people equally, regardless of social standing. To Him, all people without exception, Dalits or rich, are precious—so precious that He died for every single one of them. Whoever believes in Him, regardless of nationality or social standing, receives eternal life and becomes a son or daughter of God.

Regardless of caste, religion, or nationality, the Good News is brought to all. It is true that fewer high-caste Indians come to the saving knowledge of Christ, but the door is open for them as well.

Thomas Mathews purposed to faithfully follow God's methods for reaching the most unreached to proclaim the love of Jesus. Making disciples—*apprentices*—after conversion and then planting churches to nurture the "babes" was not a technique he stumbled upon. Rather it was the belief that Jesus intended that very thing when He gave the command not just to go, but also to make disciples and teach them as well.

God is the One Who always has and always will be building *His* Church. Mathews did leave an enduring legacy to the people of northern India, but paths through the forest are blazed for others to walk on. It is true that if not one person found Christ after Mathews died, the achievement of his forty-three years of labor would be monumental. But remember: northern India has 700-plus million people. Therefore, the 250,000 believers touched by the NMM ministry for Christ—a number far smaller than one-half of one percent of the population of the North—is only a proverbial drop in the bucket to God, who desires that *all* should find salvation in Christ Jesus.

Mathews himself understood this great need and his own limitations early on. As a twenty-year-old young man he had pleaded to God for "a handful of North Indian young people." He said to God, "I can tell them about what You have done for me, and I can teach them the Bible and disciple them. *Then, they can continue the work better than I would be able to do.*" Jesus told His disciples, "Unless a grain of wheat falls into the ground and dies, it remains alone; but if it dies, it produces much grain" (John 12:24). Mathews knew that many "grains" would need to die to themselves and allow the power of Christ to flow through them in order to accomplish God's plan to save northern India.

From the Lord's apostle, Thomas, in A.D. 52, to Mathews' mentors, P.M. Philip in the South and K.V. Philip in Rajasthan; from William Carey to Amy Carmichael; other grains of wheat had spent their lives for the spread of the Gospel in India. When the work began to flourish, Mathews had no doubt that he was standing "on the shoulders of giants"; that it was not *his* work that had brought about such results.

A Time of Transition

When Mathews died, the grief that comes with loss, mingled with the joy of knowing that he was with Jesus, colored the first days after his death. The funeral was a glorious "home going," with love poured out toward the family from all over the globe. This humble factory worker's son had gained access to thousands of hearts because of his caring, compassionate servant's heart. He would be missed.

The loss of such a dynamic, dedicated leader often leaves a void in spiritual endeavors such as mission work. But the transition had begun years before, so the road ahead had already been paved. The humility of Thomas Mathews had opened his eyes to the simple fact that he was only one man in God's great plan for northern India. If he proved unfaithful to his calling, or if he should be removed because of sickness or death, someone else would fill the gap.

God gave Mathews the vision of a team ministry concept several years before he died. He then encouraged other pastors and missionaries to take a more active role in the leadership. Finally, he began to divide the responsibility. When he went home to be with Jesus face to face, a structure was in place and functioning that could meet the mushrooming demands of NMM expansion.

His own family was included in this vision. Indeed, today each member fills a vital role in the NMM ministry that was nurtured by Mathews up until the day he died. Mary still carries the same passion for the Lord and for people that she shared with her husband. She constantly travels to the villages, encouraging the ladies and NMM missionaries. Whether teaching and working with the women students at the Bible school, or assisting visitors from other states or countries, Mary continues to serve and to be available to help those in any need.

Many years ago, God changed Mary's heart and gave her a vision: "For one mother, I will give you thousands and thousands of mothers in North India... Through you I will save thousands of souls. Get prepared, for I have chosen you for My ministry." That vision has not dimmed. Not only does she now have thousands of spiritual mothers, she herself is a spiritual mother to countless numbers of grateful North Indian "daughters."

The Mathews' oldest daughter, Grace, serves the Lord along with her husband, Joy Punnoose. After Pastor Thomas' home going, the NMM Executive Council asked Joy to take the main leadership position over the entire organization. Joy, Grace, and their children live in Richardson, Texas, where they promote the NMM efforts throughout North America. Joy travels to India several times each year to provide leadership and to encourage the believers in the villages and the students in the Bible college. Grace manages the U.S. office in Joy's absence.

Glory, the second daughter of Thomas and Mary, serves the Lord along with her husband, Finny Philip. Finny shares a role on the NMM leadership team, and he also coordinates the theological training wing of the Bible college. Glory coordinates the NMM schools.

Thomas and Mary's son, Paul, pastors the church at the NMM headquarters in Udaipur—the first church planted by Mathews. Paul is also a part of the head office leadership team. His wife, Christy, assists him in the ministry and also coordinates the compassion ministry wing of NMM.

The ministry of Native Missionary Movement has approximately forty senior leaders, each assigned to a different region. These senior leaders and everyone else in the NMM family make a good team because they share the same Spirit-filled vision—reaching the lost with the message of the Gospel and planting churches. More than any other reason, this explains the amazing results and the continual growth. The fruit of the ministry reproduces itself because God blesses those who follow the leading of the Spirit of His dear Son.

Chapter Twenty

NMM: Love in Action

Church Planting

$\mathcal{T}$he results of the past forty-four years speak for themselves: 1,300 churches established in northern India along with another 250 satellite churches (those in the process of becoming a recognized church); embracing 250,000 vibrant Christians who meet together to worship the Lord, learn from His Word, and encourage one another.

Amazing statistics, aren't they. But what do statistics mean to the *five hundred million* people of northern India who have never, that's right, *never* heard the name of Jesus? The colossal task of bringing the joyous news of peace on earth to those hundreds of millions remains to be finished.

These figures, however, do reveal much hope, for they represent an effective strategy for winning the North. Those who have been born again are taking their relationship with Jesus seriously and are eager to be a part of the soul-winning team. They long to see friends, neighbors, and relatives experience the peace and joy that living for Jesus brings to them. This commitment to the lordship of Jesus in a believer's life that

Native Missionary Movement churches preach and teach fuels the fires of salvation for the North.

The churches that Native Missionary Movement missionaries plant in each culture are indigenous in character, self-governing, self-propagating, and, within a short time, self-supporting. In every NMM church, great emphasis is placed on love, worship, teaching the word of God, prayer, fellowship, and missions. This has resulted in a loving, compassionate, and bold witness for Christ. The missionary training centers reap the fruit of this as well, for up to 90 percent of the students come from these churches.

All NMM church planting is based on the love of Christ. Here's one way in which a new church was born.

Raman Bhai was stunned when he answered the door and found several pagan priests standing outside. Immediately, warning bells went off in his mind. After all, to them he represented the competition! However, even more surprising was their request: They asked the native missionary to pray to his God for a critically ill girl from a non-Christian family. After they realized that they could not heal her with their chants and rituals, they had brought her along to save time.

What had made these priests willing to humble themselves, admit their lack of power, and seek help from the Christian God? A few weeks earlier, the girl's brother had fallen seriously ill, and her parents had summoned different priests to offer prayers and animal sacrifices to their gods for his healing. However, when all their efforts proved vain, the family priest finally washed his hands and left their home. As a last resort the parents invited Raman Bhai to pray for their son. That had resulted in his complete recovery.

Now Raman perceived that God wanted to show not only these priests but also the entire village that, indeed, He was the only true and living God. So Raman agreed to pray for the girl as well.

It was a strange "prayer meeting" that the young native missionary found himself in. He alone called upon Jesus, while his unusual visitors stood right beside him to watch what his God would do. The Lord in His faithfulness answered His servant's prayer in a powerful way, and the sick girl was miraculously made whole.

No doubt the priests and the people of this rural village in Gujarat, India, saw a "Great Light." God in His love was drawing people to Himself. Both of these children that the Lord healed believed in Jesus as their Savior, and the church brother Raman Bhai had planted in this area grew to a point where they no longer could fit in a private home.

Everyone rejoices and praises God when a new church is born in an unreached area like this one. Through the power of the Holy Spirit, the number of believers will multiply and the church will become that city "set on a hill" Jesus talked about in Matthew 5:14. And indeed, it is only a matter of time before new fellowships like this one become clearly visible to the community—and to their enemies. That is when they must move from a home into a larger, rented facility to accommodate all the church members and visitors.

Though a joyous occasion, it is often also the beginning of serious problems and persecution. Angered by the presence and activities of the church, anti-Christian individuals and groups persecute the believers and threaten visitors and seekers who associate with them. In addition, they put serious pressure on any present or future landlord until he cancels their lease. This forces the church to move from one place to another until they run out of options.

It is very difficult for a pastor to build a solid work under such adverse circumstances. Even if his congregation stays faithful, the situation is less than inviting for any potential visitors. The greatest need for such a harassed church is to have a place of its own where believers can worship Jesus in peace and grow in their faith without constant interference. The very best thing is if growing congregations such as Brother Raman's can build their own church house and not have to rent at all.

Dozens of churches have reached this crossroad today and are in desperate need of a building. The average cost of a simple concrete and brick structure that reflects the local culture and seats 250 people (on the floor!) is $5,000. It seems amazing that such a building could be constructed for such a small amount, but for many of these young churches in North India, $5,000 is a lot of money, far more than they have the ability to raise on their own.

The believers in these churches willingly and eagerly work as much as they possibly can on the construction of the building. They also donate as much toward materials as they can, but the cost of the land on which to build is often beyond what they can afford. Praying and trusting in God, they wait for Him to provide the funds for the land, and then to provide the funds that they need to complete the building.

Bible Schools

Reaching the most unreached in North India: That is Native Missionary Movement's God-given vision. NMM realized years ago that they would need to send out hundreds of pioneer missionaries to begin church planting in North India for this vision to become a reality. To date, God has enabled NMM to train more than 1,200 missionaries.

The goal of this training is to instill in each student the same vision of reaching the North by sharing the Gospel, making disciples, and planting churches. The teachers at the Missionary Training Centers provide on-the-job training with this goal in view through ongoing outreach ministry. They give quality instruction in the Word of God and prepare the new missionaries for pioneer work, hardship, persecution, and a life of faith in Jesus.

Apart from their studies, priority is given to personal character building and prayer. Ninety-eight percent of the graduates minister in places where the Gospel has never been preached before. Frequently, graduates will establish a fellowship within their first year on the mission field.

Filadelfia Bible College, a fully accredited school, graduates scores of passionate students every year. These graduates are joining the rising tide of the thousands who are preaching liberty in Jesus Christ from the bondage of Satan to the millions in the North.

What difference can just one missionary make in this land of spiritual darkness? The story of Heeralal Bhai will give the answer.

Heeralal Bhai belonged to the Mina people group, one of the largest and least evangelized tribal groups in Rajasthan. Along with his wife, Sardari, and six children, he worshipped several gods and goddesses. Little did he know what God had planned for him.

Due to a tumor in his spine, he became completely paralyzed and totally bedridden. Knowing that four of his relatives had died with a similar illness, he was overwhelmed with fear. His family members carried him on his cot to the village sorcerer, but the sorcerer performed all his rituals in vain. Then Heeralal was taken to various hospitals for medical treatment, but nothing brought any change in his condition.

One day Heeralal's sister told him about a native missionary from a neighboring village who had prayed for her son, and the boy was healed. Heeralal was desperate to meet this native missionary, so his sister arranged a meeting at her house. Again, four of Heeralal's relatives carried him and this time brought him to his sister's house. The missionary shared the Gospel with them and prayed for him. Much to the disappointment of Heeralal's relatives however, there was no change in his physical condition. But by the end of the prayer, he gave his heart to Jesus!

Heeralal was filled with indescribable peace, and he decided to follow Jesus. Now eager to attend church and learn more from God's Word, he asked his people every week to help him get to the church. For several weeks they carried him back and forth to the neighboring village. One day, with the help of four people, he was lowered into the water and baptized as a public testimony of his faith in Jesus.

Soon Heeralal's relatives deserted him, having grown tired of carrying him around. But his wife faithfully continued to take care of him. She also had the responsibility of running their store, farming, and taking care of the six children. She alone helped him with his personal care, doing his feeding and lifting. In spite of all this hardship, her love for her husband did not fade.

In time he was brought to Udaipur, where the NMM family prayed for him. Mathews then consulted surgeons concerning Heeralal's condition. They advised that it would be risky to do surgery for the removal of the tumor. But the church continued to pray for Heeralal, and the operation was performed. Before long, Heeralal was able to move and then walk. The surgeons themselves were amazed at what had happened.

Right after the healing surgery, Heeralal dedicated his life for the ministry. He started sharing the Gospel, and his fellow villagers began to respond. Today in his own village he has a thriving church with over 250 believers!

That one missionary, sent by God at the right time in the right place, made a difference in not only Heeralal's life, but also in the lives of those 250 new saints. But the story will not stop there. God only knows how many more faithful ones will enter His Kingdom through the love and reaching out of these Christians in Heeralal's village.

The cost of covering the basic needs of one of these native missionaries ranges from $50 to $100 a month, depending on the location he is working in, as well as the size of his family. This small amount enables the missionary to devote his entire time to preaching the Gospel.

Just think, a family can spend $30 or more for just one evening out at a restaurant or at the movies. That same $30 can help support a native missionary who, in one month, can share the Gospel with hundreds, perhaps thousands, of people. A meal out lasts only until we are hungry again; but helping people come to know Jesus as their Savior will satisfy their spiritual hunger for eternity. What a wonderful reward it is to have a direct part in winning thousands of souls to the Lord Jesus Christ.

Native missionaries like Heeralal are willing to go and, if called upon, even to lay down their lives. All they need is someone to send them. Sending a Gospel messenger out to an unreached village so the people there can hear about salvation through Jesus Christ could be your greatest opportunity to serve Him.

Just as Mathews did not convert all the North India Christians himself, the missionaries who follow in his footsteps are not doing the work alone. They, too, are simply kernels of wheat. The ones they reach are reaching out to others themselves.

The remarkable thing is that the Spirit of Christ is moving in the hearts of new Indian believers so mightily that many are waiting and longing to go out as missionaries. They consider it joy to be sent out, even in the face of hunger and persecution. The sad thing is that the meager support with which they are willing to get by is often not available. A huge army has been raised, the soldiers are ready to march, but the money to send them to the battle is wanting.

Literature Production

Gospel tracts printed in native languages are one of the most powerful tools on the Indian mission fields. People do not throw them away but eagerly receive and read them, and then pass them along to others. For millions, such tracts will be the only source for learning about salvation through Jesus.

Even in a land where literacy is woefully low (the number of literate people in Rajasthan hovers around 40 percent), people will eagerly take Christian literature and hide it away in a dry place, hoping that someday someone they trust can read it to them.

Because of its effectiveness in reaching the masses, Gospel literature is the number one need on the mission field. In Rajasthan, NMM operates a printing press in order to keep up with the ever-increasing need for tracts, booklets, and other evangelistic material. NMM is one of the largest literature-producing agencies in North India. More than one hundred new evangelistic book titles were released in the last fifteen years.

What is literature doing today for Christ and His Kingdom? This account illustrates just how powerful the printed word can be.

When Kalu stretched out his weary hand to pick up the half-torn piece of paper, he didn't have the foggiest idea that he was about to make the find of his life.

He carefully flattened out the crumpled leaflet and held it in the rays of the streetlight above. The title "From Death to Life" grabbed his attention immediately, and he read on. He had no idea that it was a Gospel tract. He was a high-caste Hindu from the state of Gujarat, and he had never heard about Jesus.

Every word of the simple Gospel message penetrated deeply into his heart; and as he finished, its hope moved him to cry out to this loving God. Right there, sitting in the dirt, Kalu asked Jesus to forgive his sins, and also to heal him from cancer. Immediately after he finished praying, he felt a wonderful peace in his heart. All his fear was replaced with a joy he couldn't explain.

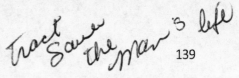

When the sun finally came up that morning, Kalu shuddered, realizing that he would have been dead had he not found the tract. He had learned several weeks earlier that there was no longer any hope for recovery from this dreaded disease, so he quietly decided to take his own life. His plan was to go to a place where no one knew him, drink poison, and die in order to spare his wife and four children the agony and shame of his suicide.

It was on that very day—in the pre-dawn darkness of a crowded city in far-away Rajasthan—as he looked for a spot to end his life, that he sat down beside the streetlight and found life, instead.

It is hard for us to imagine, but in third world countries people are very hungry for literature, especially in places where education is available. Once people learn how to read, they devour every little piece of written material they can find. Yet because reading material is scarce, most of the time their minds are left hungry. That's why one little Gospel tract can have a far-reaching impact. Not only one person but many will read it over and over.

The printed page is vital to reach the masses of India. Tracts introduce the Gospel, and they also reinforce the message people may have heard before. Each year NMM missionaries are supplied with millions of Gospel tracts in many different native languages. The cost of producing ten Gospel tracts is about five cents—less than the cost of the gum your children may buy from the gum machine in front of the local grocery store.

By the way, the wonderful story of Kalu did not end beside the streetlight. That same night he met a team of native missionaries who gave him a copy of the New Testament. He went home to his village in Gujarat a new man—and also miraculously free of cancer by the Hand of the Living God.

Through one Gospel tract Jesus found entrance not only into one heart, but also into a heretofore totally unreached village through Kalu's testimony—proof that one Gospel tract in India can indeed have a far-reaching impact.

"How sweet are Your words to my taste" (Psalm 119:103).

While Bibles and New Testaments are plentiful in the West, a church in India is fortunate to have just a few among its members. New believers desperately need the Word of God.

Imagine that you are a pagan living in a remote mountain village in northern India. Just a few minutes ago you called upon God whose name you read about for the first time just an hour ago. You earnestly asked Him to forgive your sins, and in return you made Him the Lord of your life.

Now that you have finished your prayer, you are shocked by what happened to you so suddenly. You are overwhelmed by a wonderful peace. You feel light and free from your sins. All the fear that haunted you for years is gone. Instead, there is an unexplainable joy in your heart.

You walk down the street and meet your bitter enemy. To your amazement you discover that you no longer hate him, but actually *love* him. Right at this point you know that the native missionary told you the truth when he shared that Jesus is the true God; that Jesus not only saved you, but also came to live inside you when you surrendered your life to Him.

You suddenly stand still, look down at your body, and try to comprehend that God Himself has actually come to live inside of you. A thousand questions come to your mind, all at the same time: *God has come to live inside me; what am I going to do now? Who is He? How do I please Him? What does He want? Do I need to bring Him offerings? How do I worship Him? How can I learn more about Jesus?*

You get an idea: *Why not write a letter to the address on the paper I read? Surely these people can help me!*

letter

So you write,

Dear Sir

I am from a Hindu family. I prayed to Jesus exactly as it said on the paper I read. I know Jesus came into my life. Tell me what I should do now. Please send me the Holy Book of the Christians.

You mail the letter, and then you wait in anticipation, hoping the postman will deliver a Bible so that you can learn about the wonderful God that has come to dwell in you.

Every month, thousands of precious people are being born again everywhere on Indian mission fields. God's Spirit is moving mightier than ever before. Yet almost all of these new believers come from a heathen background, with its multiplicity of gods. They have no knowledge of the Scriptures to instruct them. *God became a man? God lives inside me?* Everything is totally new.

Their greatest need is to know the Word of God; but how can they know it without having a Bible, or at least a New Testament?

The native missionaries continually ask for more Bibles and New Testaments for distribution to these new believers, as well as to seekers. At the time this was written, 60,000 Bibles, and 50,000 New Testaments were needed. The numbers are surely greater as you read this account.

God's desire is for the earth to "be filled with the knowledge of the glory of the Lord, as the waters cover the sea" (Habakkuk 2:14). Who will help fulfill the desire of the heart of God? Who will give these new brothers and sisters the very tool that will open their eyes to see Jesus more clearly? Who will help them to become mighty and powerful witnesses of the love of Christ?

Children's Homes and Schools

The first children's home was founded by NMM over 25 years ago. Today twelve children's homes in seven locations care for the needs of over 500 little ones. Almost all of these children are from very difficult home situations. They are given shelter, food, schooling, and spiritual care. NMM's vision is to raise up a generation of children who will discover their worth in Jesus Christ and who will have hope for their future.

Through NMM's *Sponsor a Child* program, people can meet the needs of individual children in the children's homes and schools. Due to lack of facilities and resources, no space is available at the present time to house more needy children.

NMM Schools

It is eight o'clock on a bright morning in the northern India village of Navapur, Maharashtra. Children at an NMM primary school start the day with a song, their voices sweetly mingling as one. After settling into their places, they review simple phrases in English and practice their numbers. In the hardworking communities of Mauchi and Gamit, where many are illiterate, this school gives everyone reason to hope for better days.

In 2003, NMM established ten such primary schools across India. English Medium Schools, as they are called, are conducted almost exclusively in English, and provide an atmosphere that nurtures children in mind and soul.

Compared to the general population of India, the progress of schooling among tribal children has been relatively poor. Some parents do not see the value of educating their children, especially if they did not have the benefit of schooling themselves. With 80 percent of these tribal groups living below the poverty line, many parents need the income their children can earn by working alongside them in the fields or in factories. Those children who are fortunate enough to attend school are taunted by their peers, or even assaulted by higher-caste children.

NMM's English Medium Schools are located in different tribal communities, usually where there are no other schools nearby.

They are open to any child, regardless of caste. An English language education not only gives children a global perspective, but also opens the door to opportunities they would otherwise be denied: higher education and better job prospects.

Most schools offer grades one through eight for boys and girls up to age fifteen. Because of the urgent need for instruction, classes are currently held in rented facilities. Long-range plans include the construction of school buildings as soon as funds are available.

A Key to the Community

Each school has anywhere from 100 to 300 students, usually with five to ten teachers. Teachers come from the ranks of native missionaries, members of NMM churches, or NMM Bible school students. Three Bible school students helped set up a school in a remote village in Rajasthan, where the nearest public school was more than twelve miles away. In the larger picture of NMM's church-planting work, each of these schools is a key that unlocks a community so NMM workers can share Christ's love with parents and others.

An example of that process at work can be seen in the ministry of Veeram and his wife, an NMM missionary couple in the state of Rajasthan. When he first went from house to house to promote his plan for a primary school, parents found it hard to believe anyone sincerely cared about the welfare of their children. After much prayer, he finally won the adults over and started an English Medium School that today instructs nearly 250 students.

The impoverished and oppressed people of a different village in Rajasthan received yet another amazing and unexpected benefit from establishing a school. As a result of being exposed to the Gospel through their children, nearly 200 believers worship today at a newly planted church there. Truly, "a little child shall lead them" (Isaiah 11: 6).

NMM Compassion Services

NMM's Compassion Services bring Christ's love to the suffering and needy in very practical ways. NMM missionaries and volunteers assist survivors of natural disasters by providing food, water, medical care, clothing and even shelter. Teams also minister to slum dwellers and leprosy patients in some of India's major cities. And all is done with a clear Gospel witness.

One of the much-needed services NMM provides is through a ministry called "The Well Project." Our mighty God is very creative in His methods of telling the lost about Jesus, if we are sensitive to His prompting. For example, Jesus used the backdrop of a well in Samaria to bring the Good News of His salvation to a woman drawing water. Here's an account of how God is still using the same method today, 2,000 years later!

When native missionary Kesa Bhai of the Bhil tribal group began sharing the Gospel in a remote village in Rajasthan, he received this dire threat from angry villagers: "You cannot bring this Christian religion into our village and corrupt the minds of our people. If you don't stop doing this, we'll cut you in pieces." And relations didn't exactly improve when the first villagers received Christ as their Savior. They were hated, branded as low castes, and treated as dirt.

But perhaps the most serious consequence for the new believers was that they weren't allowed to draw water from the public well. This was a tremendous hardship during the hot, summer months for these new Christians because they were now forced to walk many miles to a neighboring village. It was especially burdensome for the women, who had to carry full, heavy water pots home on their heads.

In spite of the animosity and terrible opposition, however, the number of believers increased. More than a hundred people gathered for worship each Sunday, and sometimes there was not even enough room for everyone inside the hut where they met.

As they grew in number, God rewarded the faithfulness of these dear brothers and sisters. A friend of NMM heard about this desperate need of a water supply and came to their aid. By sponsoring the drilling of a well for these believing villagers, he identified himself with those whom the Lord spoke of in Matthew 25:35, 40: "I was thirsty and you gave Me drink...Inasmuch as you did it to one of the least of these My brethren, you did it to Me."

Imagine the joy of these Christians when they pumped the first streams of refreshing water from their own well—a gift from the Lord and from the body of Christ. And just try to picture the amazement of their "enemies" when the believers invited them to draw water freely from the well!

Within the first few weeks, the hostile attitude of the other villagers began to diminish. As they drew water for themselves (and their cattle also), they became friendlier and began to interact with the believers. Now the door was opened for Kesa Bhai and the other believers to build relationships. Soon these young Christians told those villagers who had hated them and refused to listen about the Good News of Jesus themselves, sharing about the Well of water that springs up into everlasting life.

Since that first well project, the Lord provided NMM with the funds to drill ten additional wells for desperately poor Bhil slum communities, which are often devastated by drought. Each village well has an inscription placed by the well that encourages those who draw water to ask believers for an explanation. The inscription reads: "Jesus Christ says: 'Whoever drinks of this water will thirst again, but whoever drinks of the water that I shall give him will never thirst'" (John 4:13–14).

Not only did the woman whom Jesus talked to believe in Him, she went and told others in the city of her encounter, saying, "Come, see a Man who told me all things that I ever did" (John

4:29). In every village where NMM drills a well, the cycle repeats itself: the gift of clean water greatly improves people's health; it contributes to the development of their communities; and hearts are opened to the love of God. Then those new believers share the gift of Living Water with others. Because the wells are drilled near the church, believers are often readily available to share the Gospel with those who come.

There are literally hundreds of villages where the local church has yet to receive a well. NMM awaits the generosity of other friends who are willing to provide $800 to $1,000 necessary to drill one. Funding a village well produces a lasting impact for the Kingdom. It will not only bless the people with clean, safe water, but will also provide a powerful testimony that daily points hundreds to Jesus, the Savior of the world.

Consider this: Jesus promised a reward to those who give a cup of water to one of His followers. Today, through a village well, you can provide a river of life to an entire village in His name!

Medical teams

The health care needs of the poor villages and people groups are profound. One of the main causes of sickness in these communities is lack of hygiene. Medical professionals from the NMM ministry visit these people groups regularly and give health education. They teach the importance of hygiene, disease prevention, and water purification. They also teach HIV awareness, help with tuberculosis eradication, and provide other services as well. When the team first showed one of the communities the technique of hand washing and demonstrated it on one of their children, they were surprised to see the difference.

The medical team does free health screening and refers patients to the local hospital if needed. They distribute free medicines and vitamin supplements. From time to time, free dental camps are conducted. People from far and wide come to these camps for medical or dental treatment. This in turn has opened a door for the Gospel to be shared in those communities. After each camp, Bible school students and missionaries then do follow-up ministry.

Mobile Team Ministry

Mobile teams courageously venture with their vehicles into the heart of pioneer areas where the Gospel has never been preached before. They are on a dangerous and unpredictable mission, where their faith and commitment are challenged every single day. The phrase "living on the edge" accurately describes their lifestyle. Sometimes they are received favorably; other times, they barely escape with their lives. Yet their ministry has brought hundreds to Christ and has revolutionized church-planting strategy.

Brother Joseph and his team traveled 300 miles in nine exhausting hours to reach a remote tribal village in the Indian state of Madhya Pradesh. Not knowing what to expect from the villagers, they began an open-air meeting. A sizeable crowd quickly gathered, attentively listening to the testimonies and messages the brothers presented. It was the villagers' very first encounter with the Gospel, and the missionaries wondered how much these dear people understood.

Joseph, however, counting on God's mercy and the power of His Word, gave an altar call at the close of the meeting. What happened next was beyond anything the team had thought possible: forty-nine people came forward and sincerely gave their lives to Christ. That same evening the native missionaries held a Bible study for the villagers, who joyfully and eagerly received the Word of God into their hearts. All of them told the brothers in the end: "We are ready to confess our faith in Jesus publicly."

Back in the vehicle en route to the next village, the brothers were filled with joy and thanks—forty-nine villagers had just received Christ! A missionary living in a village nearby would soon follow up with each new believer and establish a mission station there.

In another village, a woman came to Christ after reading a New Testament that one of the mobile team members gave her. Transformed by the Word of God, she began to reach her own people. Soon more than a dozen people were attending a meeting in her village every Wednesday night, taught by the new local pastor.

In still another village, when the team members shared the message of the cross with a Hindu family, the entire household listened intently. The father had been ill for a long time, but as the team members prayed for him, he recovered totally from his sickness. As a direct result of their testimony, a fellowship soon started in that village.

If it ended with the team leaving behind new believers in remote locations by themselves, the fruit would not remain. The team knows that discipleship is the key to building a church; and that is why each local pastor is as much a crucial part of this effort as the team itself. A local pastor from a nearby village stays in touch with each person who comes to Christ as a result of the mobile team's visit.

In the past, the main reason that NMM equipped native missionary teams with vehicles was to make them move faster, be more effective, and enable them to reach faraway villages that otherwise would have to wait years to hear the Gospel. This is still very much a part of the plan. Yet the strategy our leaders have developed over the past few years has greatly increased their effectiveness and revolutionized our approach to systematic church planting.

Mobile teams no longer function as "lone ranger" outreach units of local churches or Bible schools. Instead they have become servants to all the missionaries, churches, and believers scattered over large areas. Their unique ministry enables pastors and churches to closely network together in reaching every village of their district.

These traveling teams consist of seven or eight members specifically trained in pioneer outreach and mass evangelism methods. They carry in their vehicles films on the life of Christ, projector kits, generators, Gospel literature, and musical instruments.

Through the careful area-wide planning of field leaders, teams are deployed to assist one missionary after another with major outreach programs such as systematic village evangelism, film presentations, and special youth and Sunday school programs. Their mobility enables them to include the surrounding villages in these ongoing events. Another major part of this strategy is to involve the local church in the outreach program, training the believers in evangelism through their example.

During the Bible school's summer outreach program, mobile teams travel with the students to spearhead their pioneer efforts, supply literature, and effectively coordinate their efforts with native missionaries on the field. The result is tremendous.

The Power of Film

Showing an Indian-made film on the life of Jesus is one of the most effective ways to share God's love with North Indian people. The film depicts the life of Jesus, and clearly shows how Jesus died for our sins. Tens of thousands give their lives to Jesus Christ every year as a result of watching this moving account. Five film teams move about the North continuously, showing the film and doing follow-up discipling.

Watching a movie is considered entertainment for much of the world. But in underdeveloped countries such as India, the "Man of Mercy" film is being used to bring Jesus to thousands of hungry, illiterate souls. This true story illustrates the power that God can unleash through the medium of film.

A highly unusual and potentially dangerous request shocked a native missionary mobile team one day. They had received an official invitation to come and show the "Man of Mercy" film. To be invited anywhere was unusual in itself, but the place where they were to show the moving account of the life of Jesus was none other than the local Hindu temple! Since it was festival time, more than one thousand people were expected to be there to worship the Hindu idols.

Although the opportunity excited them, the team had cause to be wary. In the past, fanatic Hindus in other locations had often tried to stop the film's showings, sometimes destroying the equipment and beating up the evangelists. Would this time be any different?

There was much potential danger involved. But on the other hand, sharing the love of Jesus Christ with more than one thousand lost men, women, and children was worth the risk. The team courageously accepted the invitation. They continually thanked the Lord for this glorious opportunity, in spite of what might happen.

The day of the festival came, and the team arrived at the crowded temple and set up their equipment; then the projector was turned on. The people watched intently and listened quietly. But the greatest surprise came after the film was over. When an invitation to receive Christ was given, thirty-eight people responded, right there on the temple grounds! One man in attendance even invited the team to conduct a weekly worship meeting in his house.

When talking about this wonderful event, one of the team members reflected, "If we wouldn't have had a film, they wouldn't have allowed us to enter their temple gate." Instead, much to the team's amazement, no one opposed them. It was a miracle!

How God used them is a great example of how He can bless any one of us when we respond to His leading.

Mission leaders unanimously report that this film is the single most effective tool they have to gain entrance into those villages, schools, and communities that otherwise would never allow any kind of Gospel work. The film draws thousands of non-Christians. Often the entire village will come out, and when they do they see and hear the Gospel for almost three hours. This powerful tool is especially effective for reaching illiterate people and those who have never had any kind of introduction to Christ.

Since this movie is produced in India using Indian actors, the audiences can easily identify with and understand its message. Jesus is no longer viewed as a Western god, but as the God who can understand them. Outreach and follow-up work are more effective after a village has seen this film, narrated in their own language.

God has blessed NMM with tremendous opportunities and tools, like this film, to win the lost. Praise God for one tribal man who had the chance to be born again at the age of seventy-eight after watching it. However, we must deeply grieve that so few of this elderly brother's generation could be reached before it was too late. We must not waste any more precious time and resources on things that pass away. Let us determine to do all we can to change the eternal destiny of millions of souls who have no hope unless we give it to them.

Navapur Convention

The hot Indian sun is just beginning its slow ascent over the village of Navapur, in the northern state of Maharashtra. This ancient land has seen many sunrises, but this day is different; a sense of anticipation fills the air. The usually quiet, dusty roads are filled with traffic of the Indian variety—cars and trucks blended together with a colorful mixture of pedestrians, carts, cows, goats, and sheep. Trailers full of rice and lentils are pulled down the winding, uneven roads to the NMM mission compound, for this is the place where all the activity will converge to a joyful climax. This is the annual convention of Filadelfia Fellowship Church of India (the church planting ministry of Native Missionary Movement), North India's largest Christian gathering of any kind.

What began in 1981, when less than one hundred believers met to learn, worship, encourage, and fellowship has mushroomed to an enormous yearly convention with more than 50,000 in attendance.

This is an important gathering, but not only for the spiritual food and fellowship it offers. This is a time of blending and understanding, for these believers represent many different ethnic groups, languages, and castes. In addition, many of the speakers come from lands far away: Australia, the Netherlands, Great Britain, the United States, and elsewhere. As these tremendously diverse brothers and sisters spiritually embrace one another, they see that God is a God who loves all mankind, whose salvation is free for all. The phrase "...All one body we,"[13] bursts into reality. A true taste of Heaven is theirs.

A vast, brightly colored canopy is erected in the fields surrounding the mission compound, and flocks of people gather underneath to secure the best vantage point for the opening night meeting. For six days 50,000 believers will join to partake of the loving ministry and hearty fellowship that flows freely here, unhindered by personal agendas.

The humility of these people is touching. Pastors and laypeople, rich and poor, young and old find themselves on common ground, sharing meals and sitting next to one another. This is striking, considering the greater society in which they live. Joined by one common purpose—to seek God and to serve others—the convention gives those gathered together a sense of what the apostle Paul really meant when he spoke to the early church of being "encouraged in heart and united in love" (Colossians 2:2 NIV).

The six days of the convention see half a million meals served at no cost to the convention delegates; over five hundred patients treated at the mission-funded medical camp; and thousands of people provided with free accommodation for the length of the convention.

In such a rich environment of expectation as this, the extent of growth and maturing which takes place in less than a week is remarkable. Conference participants have the chance to literally immerse themselves in the presence of God, living with one another in a community of faith and love. And the way these people live for the week is quite a sight to behold. Thousands at a time are served meals of rice and *dal,* a traditional Indian lentil dish, and all sit together and eat under the great canopy that is their home for the week. Their commitment to being in God's presence is moving, some traveling up to six days by bus, train, or foot in order to attend. And their diligence is well rewarded by spending the days bound together by the love of Jesus.

Ministry Needs

As the ministry of Native Missionary Movement grows, the needs increase. Many missionaries are without support, struggling to meet their family's needs and maintain their spiritual work. Several hundred Bible school students who have graduated are waiting to go to the field. But they lack support to start the work. Many villages are waiting to start schools, but due to lack of resources, nothing can be done. Resources are needed to add more film teams for outreach, to print more literature, and to provide various other ministry tools like bicycles, bullhorns, gospel flipcharts, generators, village church buildings, and wells. Providing these tools for the missionaries will make them more effective, and the work will grow faster.

Every year, many applications from young people wanting to enroll in the Bible schools are turned down, due to limited facilities and resources. The number of students could be doubled. More people must be trained soon, for the harvest is ready. NMM wants to accept more needy children into children's homes, and there are so many who need a home that they cannot be counted. Some regional leaders have already submitted requests to start children's homes in their areas. If children's homes are opened in those areas, not only the needy children will be helped but also acceptance in the community will be gained, and the ministry will grow.

Chapter Twenty-One

Suffering Saints

What does it take for an Indian of the North living under the influence of another religion to be a follower of Jesus? What does it take for a native missionary to be able to plant a church in an unreached, hostile village? It takes a willingness to lay down his or her life to follow the Savior, the conviction that the Bible is to live by, and a faith that touches God.

But no one that God ever called had all these spiritual qualities at the beginning of their journey. To be useful to Christ's Kingdom means that all self-interest has to be renounced. The mindset that Jesus revealed when he said, "I always do those things that please Him [His Father]" (John 8:29), must be the mindset of the disciple.

God deals with His servants on a personal level, transforming each one into the image of Jesus until their lives are marked by brokenness, humility, submission, and trust. It takes time, facing day-to-day struggles and experiencing God's grace, to learn such lessons. When you read about victories or persecution on the mission fields, you also encounter the personal spiritual journeys of these saints. You read how God is teaching them and molding their lives so they become useful for His service. Pray for them as they learn to serve the Lord amidst the enormous challenges to reach the unreached of their nation in this generation.

As an example, here is an amazing story of how God is using a simple, down-to-earth, Bible-believing woman to accomplish His purpose.

Anita, twenty-two years old, grew up in a jungle village in central India. Anita was seventeen when she rejected idol worship and accepted Jesus as her personal Savior. She was the only one in her family to do so. Her family members and the village people did their best to quench her desire to know more and more of Jesus. But Anita was so determined that she dedicated herself to serve the Lord for the rest of her life.

Anita faced strong opposition. When her father discovered her plan to spend her entire life preaching the Gospel, he threatened to throw her out of the house and even send her to jail. Nevertheless, Anita started to witness about the love of Jesus to her own village people. However, another confrontation was still to come.

When she finished high school, Anita asked her father to permit her to go to Bible school. When her parents strongly rejected the idea, she still wouldn't allow herself to get discouraged. She prayed often and kept her commitment to serve the Lord strong. And then one morning a wondrous thing happened: her parents relented! "If you are so determined to go to a Bible school," they said, "you may; but we will not give you a single penny!"

Hearing this, Anita jumped with joy and began packing her clothes in an old bag. Miraculously, she was given enough money to get to Filadelfia Bible College in Rajasthan, where she intended to be trained. When the village folk learned that she was going to a far-off place all by herself, many of them discouraged her. But still she stood firm in her decision to study God's Word and then dedicate herself to mission work.

In order to reach the bus station, Anita had to walk through the jungle for several hours, carrying her luggage. No one was there to wave goodbye as she left her home for the first time. There were tears in her eyes, but she possessed a great faith that God would take care of her.

During her studies, God put a tremendous burden upon her heart for a certain village, and she began to pray for boldness to witness there. She looked forward to finishing her training so she could bring the Gospel to the village of her vision.

When her schooling was completed Anita left Udaipur, ready to share God's love. There was not a single Christian in the entire village. Every morning she went out, meeting people, sharing the Gospel, and praying for the sick. God answered her prayers, and many people received deliverance from sicknesses and demon possession. Regular visits to many families with different needs paved the way for her to introduce Christ.

Within six months Anita was instrumental in bringing more than one hundred people to Jesus. Then regular worship services were started for the new believers. In time, many more villagers eagerly gathered every Sunday in a small hut for worship and to hear the Gospel.

Opposition arose right from the time people began turning to Jesus. Her opponents eyed her with suspicion because it was not common for a single lady to stay by herself in a new place and do religious work. The whole village was shaken by her faith and courage.

She was threatened many times as she traveled. At other times she was warned to stop doing Christian work. But in the midst of all this opposition, she continued witnessing about Jesus.

Persecution continued to mount. One day as the new converts were worshipping the Lord, a group of people disrupted the meeting. Someone shouted, "We will not allow such a meeting anymore in this village. You must stop it now."

But the newborn believers were not disheartened. Anita took them to another village where she saw an open door. There a family opened their house for meetings. As a result, the new converts of that village began walking several miles to attend the Bible study and the meetings in the other village because they were so hungry to learn God's Word!

After reading Anita's story, one senses that this young lady was living with a great awareness of God's call on her future. Once, when asked about her ambition in life, she answered without hesitation, "*I have no other desire than to serve my Jesus. I believe God will touch the entire village and the neighboring villages, too.*"

With great hope beaming on her face, she said, "There are thousands of people in that village who have never heard Jesus' name. I want to see everyone won for Jesus." She was willing to go, regardless of the price of suffering she had to pay.

These wonderful victories don't come without suffering paid by the native missionaries. Wherever they bring the Gospel, they first face hardship and persecution. But the winner at last is always God. Right now there are several Bible women like sister Anita who are equally dedicated and equally persecuted for their bold witness for Christ.

The largest Indian state in size, Madhya Pradesh (Sanskrit for *central state*), is located in the geographic heart of India. The 150 believers of a NMM church in Madhya Pradesh came under attack by their fellow villagers, who warned the pastor, Jorwar, not to visit homes with the Gospel. Despite this opposition, Jorwar remained strong in his faith and regularly held worship services.

One of the new Christians was a village priest who experienced God's healing touch. Many in the village were angry when they discovered his conversion. This animosity caused the former priest and his family to fear what might happen if they attended the church. Someone in the village claimed that all the spirits they worshipped had departed as a result of Jorwar's presence. Because of this, they wanted to drive the missionary and his family away. But Jorwar humbly affirmed that even if he lost everything, he would not leave the village where God had led him to share Christ. He was even willing to die for the sake of the Gospel.

Jorwar, his family, the other believers there, as well as many others elsewhere still face continual opposition after counting what it costs to be a follower of Jesus in northern India. But through the power of the Holy Spirit bringing new life to hardened skeptics such as this former practitioner of black magic, these Christians are encouraged to be strong.

What would you do if an angry crowd of people marched up to your church after a Sunday night service and shouted threats? Countless NMM missionaries face this possibility every week. Missionary Rai Singh in Madhya Pradesh was no exception.

The Sunday evening worship meeting, held in a believer's home, started out just like any other service. Rai Singh earnestly shared truths from God's Word with the gathering of about 300 people who packed the house. Little did he know that a crowd of sixty anti-Christian villagers waited for him outside.

The moment the service was over, they threatened the missionary and the house owner with drastic consequences if they continued to meet for worship. Then they severely beat the owner and a few other believers. It didn't stop there, though. They damaged Rai Singh's motorbike and tried to grab him, but people from his congregation came to his rescue. The anti-Christian group then waited a short distance down the road so they could use their weapons to beat the missionary and his wife when they passed. However, the couple slipped through a door on another side of the house and escaped.

The next day, Rai Singh, his wife, and some other believers went back to the house and prayed. This was the third growing church Rai Singh had started, and he would not stop.

A Charge From the Master

Right now there are hundreds of other dedicated native missionaries as well who are paying the price of piercing the darkness with the light of Jesus Christ. Yet no one is there to wipe their tears, comfort and pray with them, and hand them that cup of water to ease their pain. It takes so little to provide for their basic needs, since they live on the same level as the people they serve. And the return on precious souls won for Christ will be priceless.

At the time this book is being written, the persecution of Christians in India is dramatically increasing. Ultra right-wing militant Hindu groups and others are determined to stop expansion of any Christian witness in the North.

One pastor was falsely accused and jailed for three months. While in prison he led more than twenty-five men to the Lord, and another believer took his place after his release, determined to carry on the harvest.

Protesters severely beat and stabbed another brother as he preached the Gospel. Only the intervention of one of his church members saved him from death.

Sadly, some have paid the ultimate price. Aytu suffered from a serious illness for several months and found no help. But when he heard the Gospel and began attending church, he put His trust in Jesus. Then God miraculously healed his illness as well. His wife, Kosla, also became a believer.

Aytu was eager to grow in Christ, so he enrolled at the NMM missionary training center in Bijapur, Chattisgarh. He attended classes in the morning, and he worked nights for the police. He wanted to serve his Lord as a missionary after his training was completed. Kosla was learning a trade at the NMM tailoring center, also in Bijapur.

In the same town, a radical group that wages a violent struggle against landlords and government machinery actively recruited young men to their cause. But they hated Christians because believers refused to join them.

One late night in October 2007, several group members ambushed and murdered dear brother Aytu. He left behind his wife, and he also left a two-year-old son who will never know his father.

The battle rages on. What is happening in India today is reminiscent of what Paul wrote about in his second letter to the believers in Corinth:

For it is the God who commanded light to shine out of darkness, who has shone in our hearts to give the light of the knowledge of the glory of God in the face of Jesus Christ. But we have this treasure in earthen vessels that the excellence of the power may be of God and not of us.

We are hard pressed on every side, yet not crushed; we are perplexed, but not in despair; persecuted, but not forsaken; struck down, but not destroyed— always carrying about in the body the dying of the Lord Jesus, that the life of Jesus also may be manifested in our body. For we who live are always delivered to death for Jesus' sake, that the life of Jesus also may be manifested in our mortal flesh.

–2 Corinthians 4:8–11

Hard-pressed, perplexed, persecuted, struck down: What motivated Paul to eagerly, not grudgingly, lay his life on the line like this? He stated it this way: "That the life of Jesus also may be manifested in our [my] body." Or, as he says elsewhere, "For me to live is Christ" (Philippians 1:21). Anita said the same thing, so simply yet so profoundly: "*I have no other desire than to serve my Jesus.*" When a believer is full of Jesus and serving Jesus, then they can say with Paul, "I'm not crushed; I'm not in despair; I'm not forsaken; I'm not destroyed. I can do all things, because Jesus is my Strength and my Light."

Native Missionary Movement continues its rapid expansion at an ever-quickening pace. Poverty, persecution, problems all abound. But the cost is worth the sacrifice, for the eternal destiny of millions is at stake. The vision sees into the darkness of North India because Jesus is going out ahead. "I am the Light of the world; he who follows Me will not walk in the darkness, but will have the Light of life" (John 8:12).

PART FOUR:

THE CHALLENGE AHEAD

Chapter Twenty-two

Danger Ahead

*M*ountains are for climbing, even if the way is slippery and steep. Few there were who thought that the message of hope in Jesus Christ could scale the mountain of darkness in northern India that is Hinduism. But the soldiers of Light continue upward in triumph over the dark foe through the power of Him who said, "I am the light of the world"—even in the face of suffering.

The persistent persecution of the Church in North India intensifies as the army of Christian soldiers increases. But in spite of all obstacles, the combined efforts of all the Native Missionary Movement ministries and other missionary groups now produce more fruit than ever before; and it appears that the future is bright. But history has a grim reminder: Beautiful beginnings often end in dismal defeat. Seldom has any widespread movement sustained its growth over time. Sooner or later—usually sooner—Satan challenges success by causing something, even some little, seemingly insignificant thing to crop up. Then the fire begins to flicker...and finally dies; the Spirit is quenched.

Challenge is a way of life for any serious Christian, and that is certainly true of the believers in North India. Daily trials mark their walk. We have seen the cost of becoming a Christian there and what it takes to remain one. Just to be able to get food to eat is a formidable task for many of them, and the persecution, the difficulty getting places, and the lack of resources all call for unswerving faith in the mighty power of Jesus Christ.

There are, however, two dangers that loom as potentially the most serious challenges to the continued growth of God's kingdom in northern India. These two challenges pose perhaps a greater threat than any others because they come from inside the body of Christ itself.

Let's look at each of these dangers. One lurks in the shadows, waiting to subvert believers in North India; the other danger has already seduced untold numbers of Christians in the western world.

North Indian Challenge

More people live in India than in any other country in the world, except China; and in ten or fifteen years there will be more Indians than any other nationality. In northern India alone, hundreds of millions of people wait for someone to stop by the well in their village to ask for a drink and to share the Gospel of Jesus. Tens of thousands of villages yearn for a medical team to heal both body and spirit. Untold numbers of illiterate Indians desperately need to spend three hours watching the moving account of Jesus on film. Thousands upon thousands of children long for a loving home and an education.

The task that lies ahead is enormous. What will it take to reach the rest of the most unreached in India? In China? In Nigeria?

Actually the strategy for accomplishing such a daunting feat is simple. God's plan is not complicated at all. In fact to many through the ages, it has seemed too simple. Such an attitude toward winning souls, however, is not new. In every age, people have complicated the message and the ways to spread it as well.

Thomas Mathews exemplified the simplicity of the message of Christ. Mathews knew beyond a doubt that Jesus had saved him, and that Jesus was continuing to work in his life. In other words, he had a testimony of being born again and a testimony of Christ's indwelling presence to give victory day after day. He had "good news" to share with others.

Next, he had a burden to share that testimony. God gave Mathews *His* vision for the lost. He showed Mathews that He wanted to save others by using his life to show Jesus to others. So he shared the Gospel by his actions as well as his words.

When people responded to the call of Jesus, Mathews helped them to grow in Christ—he discipled them, and they began to experience the love of Jesus in their own lives. They learned that their sins were forgiven. Peace replaced fear. Many were healed of diseases. A love for others entered their hearts. Then they learned of God's plan for their lives.

As believers multiplied, a church was started so that growth would continue through teaching, fellowship, and encouragement. Finally, they were ready to comfort others in the way that they themselves had been comforted. Those babes in Christ went out and told their friends, neighbors, and the people they met in the village or at the well about the Savior themselves. Like Mathews, God "caught" these brothers and sisters, too, and now *they* had a testimony of the love of Jesus to share. Many committed their lives to go out with the Gospel themselves.

Jesus formulated and taught this strategy, and many have followed the Master's teaching. But there are other small voices that are not willing to be patient and follow Jesus' simple plan. "If we emphasize evangelism more and plant fewer churches, we can reach more people." "Better to quit witnessing, because persecution is picking up." "Concentrate on the cities. The rural people can move if they want fellowship." Pride and bickering can replace humility and love, even in the lives of the missionaries, pastors, and leaders.

The temptations are many. The voices are everywhere. Paul wrote to the Corinthians in 2 Corinthians 11:3, "I fear, lest somehow, as the serpent deceived Eve by his craftiness, so your minds may be corrupted from the simplicity that is in Christ." However, as long as NMM workers continue to emphasize listening to the still, small voice of God, the vision will not be lost, and the work will continue to grow.

Today everyone in Native Missionary Movement shares God's vision for spreading the Gospel. These workers know that they themselves play an important role in that vision. They must die to themselves and let the power of Christ love others through them. But in spite of this zeal, one thing has become clear— they cannot do it alone. The movement is expanding so rapidly and the field is so immense that, although the workers are ready to go, there just aren't enough resources to send them and keep them there. They need help. They need someone who shares the same vision.

Our Challenge

The vision of Jesus, as stated in Revelation 5:9 is to proclaim the Good News of His love to every nation, tongue, tribe, and people. This is the very same vision that is creating inroads into the darkness of North India. But in the western world, many Christians have lost their Lord's heartbeat for missions; indeed many never had it to begin with. These are hard words to hear, but they come from a God Who is loving, yet at the same time jealous for the Bride of Christ. He longs for more souls to populate heaven at the feet of Jesus.

What Happened?

"What is this?" you may say. "We have been leaders in giving to missions and going to foreign fields with the Gospel." You are right. Many from North America and the western world have given much for Jesus in foreign mission endeavors. Please read on. The past has passed. Today, the situation has changed. Let's see how.

A Misdirected Method

Long ago Christians in the west developed an erroneous viewpoint on missions that has hampered their vision. A subtle influence crept in convincing many that Christians from the developed countries held the keys to world evangelism, and they were the only ones qualified to win the world for Christ.

But today we have no excuse to continue on that line of thinking. North American believers or western believers are no longer isolated "American or western Christians." In this age of globalization, Christianity has become a global religion—just as God said it would. In fact, the center of gravity in the kingdom of Christ has already shifted to the under-developed countries. More Christians now live in the poorer nations than the more affluent developed countries. In addition, the number of new Christians there is increasing far more rapidly than in wealthy western lands. Truly all Christians are *global* Christians—all one body.

It is true that God has used believers in the United States and Canada and other places to go to the ends of the world with the Gospel. North Americans and several others have served on foreign fields and invested financial resources in missions for many years. However, after examining the moving account of Thomas Mathews and NMM, it is clear that a better way has emerged. Native missionaries are far more effective than their cross-cultural counterparts, even the ones from their own country. They know the language, and they are familiar with the customs, traditions, and religions of the people they are trying to reach. And they can reach the masses with far less expense than their foreign brothers and sisters.

Another Idol

Western Christians have given and prayed, and some have gone to mission fields. But the heartbreaking truth is that many have lost the vision of the role God wants us to play in these last days.

The vision of Jesus Christ is exploding in countless regions of the world. The opportunities to play an important part in foreign missions have multiplied accordingly, even though direct on-the-field involvement needs are fewer. With so many Christians having so much discretionary income at their disposal, we have the potential to be involved as never before.

What has happened? The answer is painful to speak, but it is clear: Countless believers have been unconsciously lured away from their love of Christ and His world vision into worshipping an idol.

O, for a closer walk with God, a calm and heavenly frame!

A light to shine upon the road that leads me to the Lamb.

Where is the blessedness I knew, when first I saw the Lord?

Where is the soul-refreshing view of Jesus and His Word?

The dearest idol I have known, what e'er that idol be,

Help me that idol to dethrone and worship only Thee.

So shall my walk be close with God,

calm and serene my frame;

So purer light shall mark the road that leads me to the Lamb.

Written by the Englishman William Cowper in the 1700's, this hymn beautifully portrays the sincere desire of someone longing for deeper fellowship with Jesus Christ. At the same time it reveals why people become ineffective in the work of the Kingdom. The blessedness of having a soul-refreshing vision of Jesus steals away. Jesus has been replaced by an idol that has become dearer.

The Hindus in India know a lot about idols. They may have dozens of them, each representing one of the thousands upon thousands of gods that a Hindu can choose to worship. These statues are usually placed on a shelf near the entrance to the home and worshipped by the occupants as they come and go.

Sadly, those of us in developed countries know about idols, too. But they are most often not the statue sort. Among all the things that we are devoted to, there is one idol in particular that we western Christians worship more than any other. That idol is self. Worshipping objects of self-fulfillment and self-indulgence take up the time, energy, and resources that are given to us by God to be used for His work. Too often in the comings and goings of our lives, we do obeisance to the idol we see in our mirrors.

The results of self-worship are disastrous for the spread of Christ's kingdom. This of course is exactly what Satan is striving for: *Get their eyes off Jesus. Keep Him off the throne.* For he knows that when Jesus is not on the throne of our hearts, then we have lost our vision, wherever we live or whatever our denominational bent. When that happens we spend our days gazing intently on our own needs, desires, and accomplishments. Our prayer lives become self-centered. We become engrossed with our own little world.

When Jesus' vision is no longer our vision, we lose His love for all mankind. Without His perception of the needs in our own neighborhood or in Nicaragua, we cannot have His compassion. We may voice a concern for the need to spread the Gospel, but our day-to-day actions reveal our true affections. When we place another object of love in our vision, it's *impossible* to love others as Jesus loves them, for our attention to the competing object of our worship has blinded our eyes and suspended the flow of the Lord's mighty power through our lives.

Losing Our First Love

The Bible bases spiritual health on the love and exaltation of the Lord Jesus, God's Son, and the love that flows from His indwelling Spirit. When Christ is loved and adored, He pours out His Spirit, and we gain His vision. When His Spirit is poured out, we love all believers, near or far, in the same way that He has loved us. By our love, everyone will know that we are Jesus' disciples. That is spiritual success. It's the same formula that has worked so well in northern India, and it produces results for the Kingdom wherever it is put into practice.

Ephesus was a city in Asia Minor. There, a cross-cultural missionary named Paul began a church. In a letter to the Ephesian believers, Paul spelled out this bedrock principle of love between believers. He said that God created us to be "holy and without blame before Him *in love*" (Ephesians 1:4). Because of "His *great love*" for us, He made us alive again—even though we were dead in our sins (2:4). The believers at Ephesus must have been on the right track at the time this letter was written, for Paul continually gave thanks to God for them because of their "faith in the Lord Jesus, and *love unto all the saints*" (1:15). True faith produces the love of Christ.

Paul stressed that Jesus Christ Himself is the foundation upon which everything is built (2:20-22). In chapters 3 and 4, Paul urged the believers to allow the Spirit to strengthen their faith in Jesus. Then they would experience the love of the Lord Jesus Christ even more deeply in their lives. When they were rooted and grounded in Christ's love, they would be filled with the fullness of God. Finally, as they became more like Jesus, they would strengthen one another in love. Then they would truly be one body.

What does being filled with Jesus look like? Paul described the indwelling Christ's effect in the second half of his letter. He said that when people are filled with the fullness of Christ, they are filled with His Spirit; they are lowly and meek; they bear with one another; they speak the truth·in love—the truth of God's eternal love; they edify one another; they are kind, compassionate, and forgiving to each other.

These are the building blocks God uses to build a church that is spiritually successful in His eyes. This is true not only of a local assembly of saints, but the full body of Christ as well. As saints do these things day by day, they are walking in love in the same way that Jesus loved them and gave Himself for them. Active, self-renouncing agape love for believers all over the world, whether in India or Nova Scotia, is the result of being filled with Jesus. It's the fruit of what His Spirit does in His disciples.

Tragically, the light of love for Christ at Ephesus, a light set high upon a hill, was snuffed out. We read in Revelation 2:4 these terrible words, spoken by the Ephesians first love, the Lord Jesus: "*You have left your First Love.*" They left the love of Jesus, and they were left without the power to love each other as He loved them. They lost the vision of reaching out with the truth of God's love to all mankind. It dwindled and died... and the light at Ephesus went out.

The tragedy of Christianity is that the tragedy of Ephesus has repeated itself over and over again, from that time to the present. We never learn from history that when we leave our First Love, we leave our only source of power to truly love each other. When self usurps the throne of Jesus and the power of Jesus' love dims inside of us, we try to love in the flesh. But then we judge; we put up walls of protection; we draw lines; we make rules; and finally we become engrossed with our own view of life, rather than being led by the omniscient vision of Christ. We have lost compassion for our brothers and sisters and have become cold.

Complacency

By their lifestyle many Christians express that life here on earth is heaven, and heaven's joy is fulfilled by meeting one's earthly desires! Tragically, multitudes have not seen that the Kingdom of God's Son is not of this world; that we are simply "passing through," as it were, as strangers and pilgrims. Self has replaced our Spirit-filled vision.

Consider the colossal increase among professing Christians in self-gratifying pleasures: high-scale food and beverage consumption; travel to exotic world-wide destinations; four wheelers, snowmobiles, jet skis—"toys" we call them; RV's, houses that rival European castles, and on and on. An increasing number worship life here and now by pouring all their energy into taking care of their flesh—at the expense of millions of eternal souls that never hear the precious news of a Savior Who for our sakes became poor. Americans are still very religious, but the testimony of millions shows that something is terribly wrong.

The churches of the West have hamstrung themselves by tagging along with the rest of society on its wild quest after self-fulfillment. The relentless pursuit of esteeming self has blinded many to the needs of a lost world and has distorted their perception of their own needs. Americans give enormous amounts to churches that, in turn, lavish tens of millions of dollars on palatial "worship centers", turn worship and fellowship in Christ into entertainment, and provide extravagant lifestyles for the "shepherds of the flock."

God has truly blessed western nations in these last times. Unfortunately, due to the bent on pleasing self, we have misinterpreted God's intentions and have used His blessings for our selfish ends. Denying self has been replaced with feeding self. Self*less* has been replaced with self*ish*.

The Church has erroneously claimed the material blessings promised by God to the physical kingdom of Israel. And many, probably most, contemporary Christians spend the vast percentage of these blessings on themselves and give little in comparison for the spread of the Gospel. Instead of laying up treasure in heaven, they lay up treasures on earth.

We cannot see what has happened because without the Lord's vision we begin comparing ourselves with ourselves, which, as Paul states, is not wise. When one Christian looks at another Christian, it is easy to find someone else who makes more, who goes more, who plays more, who spends more.

God has allowed many Christians to earn more in a month than most Indians in the North will earn in a lifetime. Often Christians here make far more money than they need to provide the necessities of life. Cell phones, multiple televisions in the home and car, swimming pools, and expensive vacations vie for a place in the family budget. Admission to prestigious colleges for the children, daily trips for lunch or lattes, and weekly trips to masseuses and tennis pros are seen by many as essentials.

"Have it your way!" Sound familiar? We are the "my way" society. Catering to people who are bent on saturating themselves with goods and foods reserved only for the rich a generation ago, producers pump out a staggering array of products. The size of grocery stores has grown accordingly with the phenomenal increase in the number of individual items to choose from. The fight over shelf space is so fierce that store chains can now charge rent on shelving for high-volume items such as breakfast cereals, chips, and soda.

This is happening in the face of abject poverty in developing nations. For citizens in these countries, often the only choice they have is whether to eat the same thing day after day or starve. Some don't even have that choice; they simply starve. Missionaries returning to the west after living in poor nations report that they are overwhelmed and depressed by the unbelievable variety in North American stores.

Western christians have deluded themselves into thinking that as long as they give something to the church or missions, whatever the amount, then they are free to spend the rest on their pleasure. God says that such an attitude is sin! "But if anyone has this worlds goods (resources for sustaining life) and sees his brother and fellow believer in need, yet closes his heart of compassion against him, how can the love of God live and remain in him?" (1John 3:17 Amplified Bible).

"If a brother or sister is naked and destitute of daily food, and one of you says to them, 'Depart in peace, be warmed and filled,' but you do not give them the things which are needed for the body, what does it profit? Thus also faith by itself, if it does not have works, is dead" (James 2:15–18).

Our affluence has desensitized us to the conspicuous needs around the world. To see a poor, homeless child on television is one thing, but could we bear to watch him or her in person living day after day begging for food, crying for love? We must wake up to the fact that the incidents and events described in this book are being played out daily—right now. Somewhere in India brothers and sisters are desperately struggling in the midst of poverty and persecution to give the Bread of Life to their friends and neighbors and loved ones.

Chapter Twenty-three

A Call to Compassion

*H*ow can we recapture the heartbeat of our Lord and His vision for those who are lost, just as we once were? The answer is clear. Jesus Himself wrote the formula, and he gave it to us in Revelation 2: 5: "Repent, and do the things you did at first." In other words, Jesus is telling us, "Go back to loving and exalting Me by loving one another in the way that I have loved you. This is why I have left you here in this sin-sick world; to show the world My image so that they, too, may believe and be saved and become My image to others themselves."

Our Lord Jesus demonstrated a heart of compassion to the lost sheep of Israel because He loved them so much. The verses above show us that if we do not have the same heart of compassion that Jesus had, then we don't have His love. We must possess true Christ-like love before we can reach the lost.

We need to see people with the eyes of Jesus. Mark 6:34 says that "Jesus...*saw* a great multitude and was moved with compassion for them." When we see our loved ones, our friends, our neighbors, our brothers and sisters in Christ wherever they are, we must see them as Jesus sees them. He loves them and He longs for them to be filled with His love and to be loving others. He laid down His life for them, and He expects us to do the same thing.

A compassionate Christian says, "You are my brothers and sisters. When you rejoice, I will rejoice. When you weep, I weep." A complacent Christian says, "Be warm and filled," but he doesn't do anything to help. The compassion of Jesus always results in self-denying acts of love.

Jesus said that there was one identifying characteristic by which everyone would recognize that people were his followers: their love for each other. And Jesus also stated the standard of that love: "...as I (Jesus) have loved you" (John 13:34). This was His commandment, not simply a suggestion. It is not optional. His disciples *will* love just like He loves them. Hungry, searching men, women, and children long to discover the love of Jesus that flows out of humble vessels filled with His Spirit.

"For you know the grace of our Lord Jesus Christ, that though He was rich, yet for your sakes He became poor, that you through His poverty might become rich" (2 Corinthians 8:9). Jesus' heart of compassion for you and for me compelled Him to become poor for us. Are we willing to reduce our lifestyle expectations so that this very same Heart, living in our hearts, can show His love for others through us?

If It Does Good, Do It!

It shocks us to realize that our religion here in the hotbed of contemporary Christianity has degenerated to the level of those we have tried to convert! We have become idol worshippers ourselves.

"Where your treasure is, there your heart will be also," Jesus states in Matthew 6:19–21. Our treasures lie all around us. Most Americans, no matter what there social standing, are inundated with material goods that, not too many years ago, had yet to be invented! Today these earthly objects have attained "must have" status, and they dominate our time and control our bank accounts. We are in bondage to self.

Do you recall the slogan, "If it feels good, do it"? We are living in the "feel good" era. This mindset drives even Christians as reflected in our jobs, our recreation, our food, our houses, our cars, our relationships, our religions—our lives. What if saying "no" to buying that bigger house made the difference for one soul in eternity? Would you say no?

We believers, instead of being driven to feel good, must immerse ourselves in *doing* good. Remember that it was said of Jesus, "God anointed Jesus of Nazareth with the Holy Spirit and with power, who went about doing good" (Acts 10:38). He went around *doing good.* If the Spirit of Christ lives inside us, do you think that He approves of us doing whatever we desire simply because it satisfies our flesh?

Jesus gave Himself for us, not only to redeem us from every lawless deed, but also to purify for Himself His own special people, *zealous for good works* (Titus 2:14). Jesus is in the business of turning us away from our *selfish* desires to *selfless* desires; to doing good everywhere we go—just like He did. These are the good works that only He can do, and He cannot do them through us if we refuse to die to ourselves.

Dethroning self is the only remedy to restore the power of Christ. God will have no other idols before Him. But when worship of self is transformed back into worship of Jesus, power is unleashed—power over sin; power in love; power in prayer; power in all areas of life—because we have returned to our first love. Jesus is our example, our pattern, our power. We must be in daily communion with Him in order for His love to flow through us. "I have been crucified with Christ; *it is no longer I who live, but Christ lives in me*" (Galatians 2:20). Jesus flatly stated in John 15:5, "Without Me you can do nothing."

The surest way to identify with someone else's deep need, even if you have never gone through it yourself, is to die more to yourself. Dying to self is the most difficult and painful process one can go through, for it goes against everything we have learned. All our lives have been built on living, on staying alive to what we know. When we die to self we experience a little of what our brothers and sisters in other lands go through when they endure ostracizing from everything they have known, or when they are persecuted in other ways, or when they face starvation.

Jesus, too, gave up everything. He became poor so that we could be rich. In the greatest act of humility ever witnessed, the love of Jesus compelled Him to become like the creature— even though the universe was His creation. He too was poor; He too was despised; He too was rejected. That's how much He loved us.

The difficult thing for us in all this is that Jesus expects us to have the same mind in this matter that He had, and still has. We are expected to possess the same heart of love!

Many Americans have helped those in need to find hope in Jesus at one time or another. But we need to be open and honest with the reality of the times and the seriousness of God's demands.

We know that everything we own comes from God, and that we are simply stewards of *His* wealth—however much we have been given. The Bible abounds with stories of those who are blessed for dealing wisely with this world's goods. The same stories also speak harshly about those who abuse what the Lord has given.

"For everyone to whom much is given, from him much will be required" (Luke 12:48). And many of us have been given much. The Bible speaks of equality among brothers and sisters. This practical application of love has been evident in the Church since the believers in Jerusalem shared what they had with one another.

Global Equality

For many years Native Missionary Movement relied almost completely on gifts from Indian people. But several years ago, the needs began to outpace the donations. Now, the eyes of more than a thousand missionaries and countless other workers are fixed on the nations of this earth that God has blessed with temporal riches.

The Christians of North India are crying out to us for wells to be dug; for bicycles and motorbikes for the pastors and missionaries; for more mobile vans and films; for more children's homes and schools; for more medical teams. The workers live a life of deprivation; the leaders live by faith and do not receive a salary. They cry out, "Who will help us win the most unreached of our homeland for Jesus?" Who will help them fulfill God's vision?

Remember: We are *global* Christians. The suffering saints in Pakistan or Peru need to be in the pool of those we compare ourselves with as well as our affluent Western neighbors. If we willingly size up our lifestyle with the abject poverty of a saint in Rajasthan, we can begin to see the picture more clearly. The "cost of living" factor has no merit in the comparison. In the final analysis it boils down to two questions: 1) Do I have more than I need for daily necessities? 2) Do other believers fall short of their needs? If the answer to both questions is "yes," then a third question must be asked. "Why am I not sharing with my needy brothers and sisters?"

When one part of the body hurts, the whole body should feel the pain, even if the hurt originates in Indonesia, India, or Ireland. When Nigerian believers experience joy, the whole body should share in their happiness. With today's high-tech communication lines, this can take place almost immediately.

The native missionaries are not looking to "keep up with the Jones's" of the world. They simply want what it takes to share the Good News of Jesus out of a heart of love and compassion.

God intends for the wealth of North America and other nations to be used for reaching every people, tribe, and language. The previous generation wondered how God could ever reach all the people groups in the world. Now all doubt has been removed. Satellites, high-speed travel, computers, and video projection bring the Gospel to millions. The impossible has become reality. But we must never lose sight of the enormous cost of reaching hundreds of millions still in darkness.

Does this mean that sacrifice is necessary for us? Let's look at what God says in His Word. Jesus spoke the first four quotations. The last one was spoken about Him.

❏ If anyone desires to come after Me, let him deny himself, and take up his cross daily, and follow Me. For whoever desires to save his life will lose it, but whoever loses his life for My sake will save it (Luke 9:23, 24).

❏ Whoever of you does not forsake all that he has cannot be My disciple (Luke.14:33).

❏ Do not lay up for yourself treasures on earth (Matthew 6:19).

❏ I am among you as the One who serves (Luke 22:27).

❏ Your attitude should be the same as that of Christ Jesus (who) made himself nothing, taking the very nature of a servant (Philippians 2:5, 7).

Yes, it takes sacrifice. But denying oneself and becoming a servant is the hallmark of a disciple of Jesus. It is the way the Master Himself went; should not the servant tread it still? These words are hard, but God disciplines those he *loves*. He has a job for us to do, and He will keep showing us how to love until we get it right. This is the way the Father loves. This is the way Jesus loves. This is the way His Spirit loves. This is the way we will love, if Jesus has free reign in our lives. In the light of these eternal absolutes, we cannot turn our backs any longer on the needs of our brothers, wherever they may be.

We were created in God's image. Our top priority is to reflect Jesus, to do what He does. God loves us the way we are, but He refuses to leave us that way, for He wants us to reach the high calling of reflecting Jesus completely. We often try to fit God into our own agenda. We must give up our agenda in order to live out His agenda.

It's too bad that missionaries on foreign fields are usually the ones in the limelight and attract all the attention. But God doesn't see it that way. To Him all believers are partners— teammates who contribute to the harvesting of souls. Everyone is a missionary to the lost around them. In addition, each believer is commanded to contribute to the needs of the Body of Christ at large as the Lord supplies. We must not only pray for the needs in our own assembly of believers, but also for those in other regions and lands. We also must help our brothers in their temporal needs as well, especially in the areas that affect our brothers' ability to spread the Good News of Jesus.

Oswald Chambers said this regarding the key to success: "The secret of the missionary is: I am His, and He is carrying out His enterprises through me."

We all are missionaries working under the same law. "I can do all things *through Christ* who strengthens me" (Philippians 4:13). "*Christ in you*: the hope of glory" (Colossians 1:27). This is the faith that is conquering the mountain of darkness in India, and it is the same faith that will energize North American and other Christians to join in the battle.

In the previous chapter mention was made of the army of missionaries that God is raising in India to go to the mission field. However, in God's perspective, that small army represents only a part of the greater army that marches forth to war. That army is called "The Bride Of Christ—the Church." That means we are all in this together. "And if one member suffers, all the members suffer with it; or if one member is honored, all the members rejoice with it" (1Corinthians 12:26).

Prayer

You bring home the unassembled bicycle on Christmas Eve. At midnight, frustrated and tired, you glance down to the floor at the pile of packing materials and tools and notice a small white booklet. The directions! All else has failed up to now; why not try them?

Prayer, like the direction booklet, is often viewed as a last-gasp help to fall back on when nothing else seems to work. How often have you heard a statement like this: "I wish there was something I could do to help. I guess all I can do is pray."

"*All I can do.*" To God, it is what we *must* do before we do anything else! Prayer is communicating with the Lord, and He is the One who will do what needs to be done, through whomever He chooses to do it.

Intercessory prayer for our brothers and sisters in Christ is not to be something we save for a prayer meeting. Paul, who implores believers to "pray without ceasing," also has the following to say regarding prayer for the spread of the Gospel and for those in need:

❑ (Pray) always with all prayer and supplication in the Spirit...with all perseverance and supplication for all the saints (Ephesians 6:18).

❑ Continue earnestly in prayer, being vigilant in it with thanksgiving (Colossians 4:2).

❑ Finally, brethren, pray for us, that the word of the Lord may run [swiftly] and be glorified, just as [it is] with you (2 Thessalonians 3:1).

❑ Therefore I exhort first of all that supplications, prayers, intercessions, [and] giving of thanks be made for all men (1 Timothy 2:1).

❑ Is prayer important? More than important, it is vital—absolutely necessary to God's work. The prayers of the saints for one another accomplish the same purposes that Jesus' prayers did when He was on the earth, for it is Jesus Himelf in us who is praying, showing His love for the needs of His children. His prayers move His Father.

In the 1700s a small band of believers from different denominations and nationalities in Europe who were escaping persecution fled to an estate in Moravia, in what is today the Czech Republic. Their religious life soon deteriorated into bickering and disputes over doctrine. One Sunday the Christian nobleman who owned the estate, and who offered them a safe haven, preached on the love of Christ and loving others. The Spirit of God moved among them and hearts were broken; confessions were made; love began to flow. Out of this love-charged atmosphere, the birth of the modern missionary movement began. This little fellowship sent out more than one hundred missionaries all over the world during the century and made a lasting impact for Jesus in countless lives.

Possibly more impressive was the home congregation's commitment to intercessory prayer for the missionaries and those to whom they were sent. A prayer vigil began when the first family departed. From that time on, prayer was raised to the throne continuously for one hundred years! The success on the field was directly related to the saints on their knees.

The Moravians' commitment to prayer revolutionized the world for Christ. Today, in these last days of opportunity to bring the Gospel to everyone before God closes the curtain on planet Earth, believing, faithful prayer still can and does move mountains. It worked for Mathews and his family. Prayer is working for Anita, for Kesa Bhai, and for countless other North Indians. The fervent prayer of those who are righteous in Christ will move the heart of our loving Father (James 5:16).

You can pray as you have never prayed before. You have read page after page of the needs of NMM workers. They need your prayers!

Giving

What does God want us to do with our money? Not the money needed for the true necessities of life, but that which, if we are open and honest before the Lord, we really don't *need*? Think about it this way: If you were a Christian living in a poor village in Colombia, Chad, or India, and you longed to see your countrymen know about Jesus, how would you want a Christian to use his/her extra money?

We must recognize Christ's requirement for being a disciple. This is basic Christianity. Jesus wants those who are willing to go all the way to love others. If a heart is willing, He will supply the power to overcome any weakness on our part.

With missionaries trained and eager to spend their lives leading others to Jesus, we cannot justify our western lifestyle any longer. Would it be possible to let the Holy Spirit use us even more than we have let Him?

Living at a lower standard of living may be difficult at first. In C.S. Lewis' Chronicles of Narnia book *A Horse and His Boy,* two talking horses of Narnia named Bree and Hwin were trying to outdistance an enemy battalion that was planning a sneak attack on the peaceful city of Anvard. Bree, a former war horse himself, was commanded by Hwin's rider, Aravis, to gallop faster so they could warn the king; although Shasta, the boy who was riding him thought, "The poor chap's doing all he can already." But Lewis added, "Certainly both horses were doing, if not all they could, all they *thought* they could; which is not quite the same thing."

But at that moment, as if being followed by an enemy army wasn't enough, they heard the snarling roar of a lion chasing them. Lewis tells the reader that "Bree now discovered that he had not really been going as fast—not quite as fast—as he could. Shasta felt the change at once. Now they were *really* going all out."

Bree opened the throttle when he sensed that the situation justified the need. Today, Satan is prowling about as a roaring lion, seeking to devour whoever he can (I Peter 5:8). We have read those words in our Bibles, yet so many of us are still loping through life, intent on pleasing ourselves. The enemy is nearer than we think. We must be honest with ourselves. Are we really doing everything possible that we can, knowing that countless lives are slipping into a Christless eternity? Or, like so many of us, are we actually doing all that we *think* we can?

Poverty may come to us someday, maybe sooner than we think. If we can't give now out of our abundance, how could we ever be like the Macedonians? They gave *joyfully* in spite of their poverty to the dire need in Jerusalem at the time Paul wrote his letters to the believers in Corinth (2 Corinthians 8:1–5). If the Macedonians could give out of their poverty, and if the widow could give her last two mites (Luke 21: 1–4), could *we* find a way to do more? Can we go "all out" for Jesus?

Some do not have the high income that others do. They may be in need themselves. This plea is not meant to place a burden on those who truly have needs. But so many only *think* they are needy, when in fact, they have much more than 90 percent of the world's population.

Going

Since native missionaries are more effective, does this mean that there is no longer a reason for western christians to go to foreign fields? Certainly not! Many tribal groups in some parts of the world have not raised up churches and discipled believers to the point where they can send out their own missionaries. They need to be trained and nurtured in this concept.

In addition, technical and vocational skills are needed in areas where there are few with such abilities to draw from. Medical personnel, Bible translators, and literacy workers, to name a few, can apply their much-needed skills for the Lord on the foreign field.

Short-term missions trips serve the valuable purpose of opening one's eyes to the realities of life in another land. A visit to another culture expands our view of the world God created, and it rivets the needs into our souls in a way that words and pictures cannot do. Coming to North India would bless the Indian believers, for they would feel your love in a close, personal way.

Meeting the Challenge

On a recent fundraising trip to the Pacific Northwest, NMM president Joy Punnoose was addressing a group of sincere believers. Having shared the NMM story the previous day, he was now challenging them to consider the Savior's example of compassion, urging them to see with the eyes of Jesus. Contemplating the apathetic condition of American Christianity, one brother asked Joy these questions. "After hearing about the success of your mission and seeing the joy on the faces of these new believers in spite of the persecution and poverty, I'm wondering: What makes the difference? What is it that they have that we are missing? What makes your churches work?"

Joy paused a long time before answering, not wanting to offend anyone, but at the same time longing to help people to see their need. At last he said simply, "It's love. Our believers love each other, like Christ commanded. We share things about Jesus for hours on Sundays as we fellowship together, to help strengthen one another. During the week, if a sister sees another sister across the street, she runs over and embraces her because she loves her with the love of Jesus. We teach the believers that to love each other is Christ's highest calling."

"Love one another as I have loved you." It's this "love one another" spirit that strengthens these believers in Christ, motivating them to reach out in love to their fellow villagers and their neighbors with the saving Gospel of Jesus.

Do you have the vision of Jesus burning in your breast? Does the persecution, the poverty, the hunger, the thirst, the imprisonment of Christ's "little ones" move your heart of love and compassion to action? Your answer carries with it the weight of eternity, for you and for millions of lost souls in northern India and around the world.

Really the two challenges facing Native Missionary Movement are one. Both the danger of NMM losing the method and North America losing the vision are rooted in self becoming an idol. Each one of us is under command to deny ourselves, pick up our crosses and follow Jesus. But, praise God, through the power of the Holy Spirit, challenges produce conquest.

What a glorious responsibility we have: to be partners with brothers and sisters around the world in the greatest conquest the world has ever known, with our King going out ahead. Souls all over the earth are marching out to set the captives free in the name of Jesus, and in the Spirit we move along in their ranks. Our eyes shed tears over the lost. Our feet trod through the villages. Our hands comfort the children. Our words heal the sick.

When we give, pray, and share the story with others, we are the eyes of Jesus, the feet of Jesus, the mouth of Jesus, and the hands of Jesus. We are being used to share the compassion of Jesus—empty vessels filled with the Spirit of Christ—just like the workers on the field. What indescribable joy will be ours to be together with them at the feet of Jesus, and with the ones who heard about Jesus because we all had His vision through the darkness.

Chapter Twenty-four

Epilogue

*I*n these last days we are witnessing the twilight of religious freedom in our land. Everywhere the signs point to less toleration of Christians and a stronger stand against Biblical principles once considered inviolate. We are now in a position to be able to identify with our persecuted brothers and sisters in India and elsewhere, at least to a small degree. The knowledge that we have a charge from our Master to keep—to share what we can while there is still time and while we still have the resources—must prompt us to action.

Martyrdom isn't an option, reserved for Christian "fanatics." The word *martyr* means *witness*, and God does not speak kindly of those who will not testify of their faith in Jesus in action as well as word. We are also called to the spirit of martyrdom.

What will happen to Native Missionary Movement? Will the vision that God gave to Thomas Mathews continue on? It will somehow, for God has promised that His Word will not return to Him void, empty. The Gospel of Christ will come to every nation, people, tribe, and language.

But how that will happen only God Himself knows. Surely the completion of the task lies not far down the road. So many events point to the end of time coming soon. Satan recognizes the victories his enemies have garnered for their Lord, and he is not standing idly by.

Reginald Heber, the English minister and hymn writer who penned "Holy, Holy, Holy," paints a beautiful portrait of the persecuted in the hymn, "The Son of God Goes Forth to War;" and in each of the first three verses, he poses a question. Read the poem carefully, for eternity is at stake.

> The Son of God goes forth to war, a kingly crown to gain;
>
> His blood-red banner streams afar: Who follows in His train?
>
> Who best can drink his cup of woe, triumphant over pain,
>
> Who patient bears his cross below, he follows in His train.
>
> The martyr first, whose eagle eye could pierce beyond the grave,
>
> Who saw his Master in the sky, and called on Him to save:
>
> Like Him, with pardon on his tongue in midst of mortal pain,
>
> He prayed for them that did the wrong: Who follows in his train?
>
> A glorious band, the chosen few on whom the Spirit came,
>
> Twelve valiant saints, their hope they knew,
>
> and mocked the cross and flame:
>
> They met the tyrant's brandished steel, the lion's gory mane;
>
> They bowed their necks the death to feel:
>
> Who follows in their train?
>
> A noble army, men and boys, the matron and the maid,
>
> Around the Saviour's throne rejoice, in robes of light arrayed:
>
> They climbed the steep ascent of heav'n thro' peril, toil, and pain:
>
> O God, to us may grace be giv'n to follow in their train.

In Revelation 3:8, the victorious Lord Jesus says, "See, I have set before you an open door, and no one can shut it." The saints in the hymn carried forth the banner of Jesus Christ, in spite of the cost. The strength of Jesus gave them power over darkness. They drank from the Savior's cup. They carried His cross. Their eyes saw what He saw. Their feet carried them where He went, through the open door into the battlefield. They were all simple people with eagle eyes fixed on Jesus.

Thomas Mathews also saw with the vision of Jesus—a gaze that looked beyond the darkness of the land into a never-ending day. That vision led him on a mission to North India, which in turn spawned a movement of thousands upon thousands of new saints in Christ's noble army. May each one of us be given the strength of our Lord Jesus Christ to march with our brothers and sisters in North India and around the world, and follow in their train.

Chapter Twenty-five

A Call to Commitment

*H*ere is a brief overview of the work of Native Missionary Movement today. It represents opportunities to show your love for Jesus and your brothers and sisters in need.

- ❑ Support a Missionary
- ❑ Support a Child
- ❑ Children's Homes
- ❑ Christian Schools
- ❑ Mobile Van/Film Teams
- ❑ Compassion Ministries: Slum Ministry, Well Project, Medical Missions etc.
- ❑ Church Building
- ❑ Printing
- ❑ Training Centers
- ❑ Bible College

For further information regarding any of these opportunities or *NMM* itself, contact:—

In the United States:

Joy Punnoose, President
821 Vinecrest Lane
Richardson, TX 75080
972–470-9707
Email: contact@nmmindia.org

In Canada:

Randy Wyton, Director
202, 10110-124th Street
Edmonton, AB, T5N IP6
Email: contact@nmmindia.org

In India:

Native Missionary Movement
Church Road, Sanjay Park
Udaipur, Rajasthan 313 004
Email: contact@nmmindia.org

❑ Keep up-to-date with NMM India. A free monthly newsletter is available. Just email or call the above number.

❑ NMM would love to share their story with your church, home fellowship, Bible study, or other gathering. Call NMM for details.

❑ Learn more about NMM on our website: nmmindia.org.

Appendix

1   From his early years on, Thomas Mathews adopted his last name as the name he went by. His parents' name of affection, "Joy," was dropped. All through the rest of his life, his friends simply called him "Mathews."

2   The language of Kerala

3   About two dollars

4   A different Chacko than the one who prayed for the healing of Mathews' father

5   "Old Delhi" as it is called, to differentiate the metropolitan area from the adjoining national capital, "New Delhi"

6   Later on Philip developed Hodgkin's disease and died, leaving behind his wife and five children. But this young man was a "grain of wheat" in the soil of Rajasthan that enabled Mathews to see the harvest later on. "He who reaps receives wages, and gathers fruit for eternal life; that both he who sows and he who reaps may rejoice together" (John 4:36).

7   In India the people never touch the mug to the lips, because water would be wasted washing it again and again. So they lift the mug up above their lips and pour the water into their open mouths.

8   Prayers

9   God

10 About $13

11 "Uncle" is a term of respect used for any older man, related or not, in this land where older people are honored and respected. Older women are called "Auntie."

12 Many of God's miracles involved postmen!

13 From the hymn "Onward, Christian Soldiers."